HIRANYAKASHYAP

BOOK 2
HIRANYAKASHYAP
THE NARASIMHA TRILOGY

KEVIN MISSAL

HarperCollins *Publishers* India

First published in India by
HarperCollins Publishers in 2020
A-75, Sector 57, Noida, Uttar Pradesh 201301, India
www.harpercollins.co.in

2 4 6 8 10 9 7 5 3 1

P-ISBN: 978-93-5357-819-0
E-ISBN: 978-93-5357-820-6

Typeset in 11/14.7 Minion Pro at
Manipal Digital Systems, Manipal

Printed and bound at
Thomson Press (India) Ltd

To all the lovers of mythology.

NOTE TO THE READER

Read *Narasimha*, the first book in this trilogy, before starting this one. Though I have given you a summary of the first book to refresh your memory, I do feel like you'll feel and care about the characters and the events in this book even more after you read *Narasimha*.

For this book, my inspiration has been solely to carry these characters and their lives forward, and inject extreme pace into it since the first book was all about building the scene.

Hope you enjoy it!

— Kevin.

THE TRIBES

DEVAS

The Devas are foreigners who come from the island of Swarg, which lies to the north of Illavarti. They usurped the northern part of the country and gained control of major cities. Their ruler is called Indra. They worship various elements of nature, like fire, water and ice. They have long lifespans – two to three hundred years. They are really fair and are often associated with the colour white. They are the creators of Somas, which is a blue medicinal liquid derived from the Somalia plants found in Swarg. They believe in Dharma as well as the Trinity Gods – Vishnu, Mahadev and Brahma.

ASURAS

The Asuras are foreigners from the island of Pataal, which is to the east of Illavarti, across the Black Ocean. They are brown-skinned, golden-eyed and worship attributes like strength and valour, rather than the elements like the Devas. They rule the southern lands of Illavarti and their capital is Kashyapuri. They are often associated with evil because they do not have a religion and don't believe in one. They do not partake of the Somas. They have a strong exoskeleton and are competent in battle.

DANAVS

The Danavs are divided into Poulomas and Kalakeyas. The Poulomas are short giants, often ranging from ten to fifteen feet, while the Kalakeyas are over twenty feet tall. They live in large towers that are specially constructed for them. They eat large amounts of food and water. They are historically blood brothers of the Asuras and live in Hiranyapur. Other than the need for constant sleep and food, they do not have a purpose in life.

SIMHAS

According to mythology prevalent in Illavarti, the Simhas were created by Lord Vishnu in his first battle against evil. The Simhas are half-lion and half-human in spirit. They wear the skin of a deceased lion. They live in Vaikuntha, the forgotten religious city of Lord Vishnu. Since the Devas are close to being on the side of Dharma, the Simhas fight the battle on the side of the Devas. They are against practices looked at as being related to Adharm. They have strong claws and their skin is pale yellowish. They have reddish beards. This Yug's Avatar is destined to be from the Tribe of the Simhas.

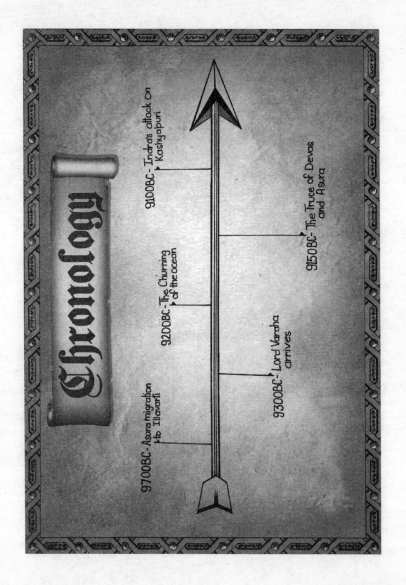

THE STORY SO FAR

Fourteen years ago, the truce between the Asuras and the Devas was broken, resulting in the death of the Asura queen.

More than a decade has passed. The instigators of the invasion in Kashyapuri have all but vanished.

As Hiranyakashyap plots his revenge against the Devas, he chooses to follow after his deceased brother's footsteps, leaving the throne to his inexperienced 15-year-old son, Prahlad, rather than his firstborn, Anuhrad.

Narasimha, a war veteran amidst the Simhas, is tormented by his past and chooses to lay low with the Manavs. But once his cover is blown, he is urged to join the third Shiva, Bhairav's cause against Hiranyakashyap's nephew, Andhaka. On the night of the first attack, he successfully vanquishes Andhaka.

Much to his disbelief, Andhaka is reported to have survived Narasimha's attack. As Bhairava ruminates over whether to use the nuclear weapon, Pashupatastra against their foe, Narasimha wonders if choosing to help these people, after all, will make him the Dharm of this age. As prophesied, the

Dharm of this age would die prematurely, leaving the fate of this world to the Adharm.

As he goes through his brother's research, Hiranyakashyap finds out that they are descended from Brahma, and are therefore heirs to the invincible armour created from the essence of Avatar Mohini. He seeks to regain the invincible armour by undergoing the Three Trials of Brahma and defeat the Devas.

The acting king, Prahlad, investigates an extremist organization, Vishnusena, running in the shadows of his kingdom. But once he realizes that the leader is Narada, a Manav noble and confidante to his deceased mother, he wonders if the organization is truly *evil*, as labelled by his aunt, Holika. He wonders if the organization's goals of religious faith would bring reforms for the Asura laws in the long run.

A horrified Narasimha, after having seen the after-effects of Pashupatastra, destroys the weapon and suggests making peace with Andhaka, much to the chagrin of Bhairav. Having won the respect of his Pride and developed feelings for one of the Simhas who nursed him, he believes he is done hiding and might be able to achieve peace without ever becoming the Avatar. As Bhairav expresses his guilt that he couldn't save his own son, they are summoned by Andhaka to make a peace treaty, on the condition that they bring the Pashupatastra.

Both parties meet to make peace: Bhairav's army and the Simhas on one hand, and Andhaka's forces, accompanied by the Asura king's brother, Anuhrad. Andhaka calls out on their bluff and reveals that he was the long-lost son of Bhairav after all. Bhairav, overcome with emotion, embraces his son, but is stabbed by him, as he declares that he is not the same hapless child anymore, but the blind prince, Andhaka. An enraged Narasimha declares war on them and accidentally kills Anuhrad. Anuhrad reveals that he had agreed to Andhaka's cause of the Asura empire's destruction, because he felt it would fulfill his vengeance, after his father had killed his true love. But then, he had realized it only brought him loneliness, even in death. He reveals that there was a reason as to why Andhaka could escape death. He asks a torn Narasimha, who feels he had killed yet another *innocent*, to protect his younger brother, who remains more virtuous than he would ever have been.

A furious Narasimha follows a fleeing Andhaka, and slaughters all of his clones. As he rams the trident of Shiva into the real Andhaka's throat, he, with gritted teeth, embraces the role of the Avatar, come what may. He confides in Chenchen, his lady love, that he was solely responsible for killing innocents back in his prime, and for leading Hiranyakashyap down a vengeful path. And now, he had claimed yet another life that was related to him. He states that his only redemption now lies in Prahlad, the current ruler of Kashyapuri.

As Hiranyakshyap barely manages to complete all three trials, he is ambushed by the army of Agni. Their onslaught bears no effect, as the now invincible Hiranyakashyap manages to make short work of them all and deliver mortal injuries to the god of fire. With his dying breath, Agni confesses that his brother, Indra, may have killed his wife, but someone else had delivered that fatal attack. That someone was a Simha, bearing the name, Narasimha.

Holika confirms her suspicion that Prahlad, might after all, be allied with the wretched organization that she had vowed to destroy. After losing her adoptive daughter in the fire caused by Vishnusena, she confronts Prahlad, whose only hope from the alliance was to bring the Asuras to the light. She kills Narada and calls for a public execution of Prahlad. She tells him that Anuhrad had died in battle, causing anguish to the young ruler. She declares that if his father would have gotten wind of his treachery, he too would have agreed with her. That death was the appropriate punishment for him. Refusing to let go of his faith in Vishnu, he is chained to rocks and immersed in the water to be drowned, amid the jeering of his fellowmen.

Andhaka is later revealed to have survived yet again, as he nears Kashyapuri.

PROLOGUE

He couldn't breathe. The very realization that he was minutes from death made him frantic, panic-stricken. He tried to struggle against his chains, to free his hands and his legs. *No. Please! Lord Vishnu, help me!*

But his eyes began to close, his lungs gave up, his limbs became numb as he struggled against the waters. That was when he felt it – two hands lifting him up from the water and on to firm soil. *Is that you, O lord?*

His ears picked up a vast cacophony of sounds, wave upon wave of just mindless noise. He was getting breathless, and the feeling of loss and failure was consuming him. In this moment, only the skies were as silent as he was. His ears were throbbing, his blood was pounding, but he was one with the skies, and the moving clouds kept account of the passage of time.

He could smell the acrid smoke of many fires, and he heard a lot of clanging iron drowning out the shrieks of civilians, their boots against the muddy floors … But these sounds gradually faded as he was dragged further away by these magical hands. *Who was it? Has Lord Vishnu come to save me?*

He couldn't open his eyes. So he kept them closed. Just for a little while.

He jerked awake. Panting heavily, Prahlad scanned the room he found himself in. He was in the centre, lying on a rocky slab, bare chested, a shawl wrapped around his body. A fire blazed in the corner, and incense candles perfumed the room.

'Calm down,' a soothing voice said.

Prahlad turned at the familiar voice to see Dhriti standing in a corner. In his panic, he just hadn't noticed the calm and peaceful Dhriti – the assassin girl who was part of Vishnusena. She was the one who had inspired Prahlad to fight against his tyrannical father. And she was the one who he had begun to fall for.

With a smile on her cherubic face, her striking red hair waving down her back, she walked up to Prahlad and stroked him on the cheek. 'I don't want you to … I don't want you to worry any longer. We saved you.'

Prahlad gazed at her for a moment. 'What? I was going to be executed. Then …'

'I brought our men to the city in disguise and attacked. We got you out and escaped into the forest and dispersed so they couldn't track our hideout,' Dhriti explained.

Prahlad nodded, clenching his jaw. He really hated his aunt right now, but perhaps she'd had her reasons for wanting him dead since her stepdaughter was killed and Prahlad was indirectly responsible for it. He knew this and he was sorry about it. But for now, his focus was right back on Dhriti who, watched him with worry.

'Thank you,' Prahlad said, rising to his feet. 'I want to see ... where we ...'

Dhriti helped him out of the hard bed, and with Prahlad leaning heavily on her, they walked to the door. He felt safe even though he looked pale, after all he had recently escaped death. He opened the door to find himself in a war camp.

The daily life of the rebels was playing out in front of him. Some were cooking, while others were sharpening their weapons. Rows of men, women and children had gathered together and were knitting and sewing various garments. Children ran around, playing with each other. The huts weren't too big, and were safely hidden under the thick canopy of the trees.

From the corner of his eye, Prahlad could see the clearing that met the cliff, overlooking the large battlefield which was on the outskirts of Kashyapuri – which he no longer belonged to. He realized that they were up in the forested hills on the outskirts of the city that still called him prince.

'Welcome to your new life,' Dhriti said, patting him on the back. 'There are a few people who want to meet you but you have been resting so I didn't disturb you.'

Prahlad nodded. 'Any new developments?'

'We lost our leader so everything is haphazard. People don't know whom to follow.'

'Narada saved me; he told me to right his wrongs. I just ...' Prahlad trailed off, arching his brows. 'Thinking about it still distresses me. But first, Dhriti, tell me – how am I still alive?'

'Lots of Ayurveda and even more sleep,' Dhriti said with a smile. 'There's something you must know though.'

'Yes?'

'We received a letter recently,' she said. 'I don't know how he found us here. But he clearly has many spies, and I'm not surprised even though it terrifies me that he knows our location. He is coming this way and wants to meet you in the next couple of days. Apparently, he wants an alliance with you. I don't trust him, but ...'

'Who are you talking about?'

'Your cousin,' responded Dhriti. 'Andhaka.'

1

NARASIMHA

One month later ...

The anguished cry tore through him and the forest at the same time. Narasimha froze for a moment. He was on his way to Kashyapuri, and the journey had been quite peaceful until now.

From the vantage point of his horse, he looked straight into the depths of the forest where the sound had emerged from. He dismounted and, without a second thought, began to sprint towards the sound. His ears pricked as he tried to listen to the cries, which grew louder as he came closer. What in the heavens was happening here?

His heart raced as he went through the bushes and the greenery, finally reaching the scene.

Three Pishach with their dark skin, straw-like hair and black armour had cornered a rishi with matted hair, dressed in an orange dhoti and carrying a staff in his hand, trying to protect the woman and two children behind him.

'We just need to know,' one of the Pishach said in a civilized tone, 'where the bird man is.'

'He's not here,' the rishi said in a quiet, firm voice.

'And yet the ravens speak of his presence here. He was hurt, you tended to him, and now you keep us from him. The council of Kashyapuri has pronounced his sentence – he is an enemy of the state.'

'Leave, or you will regret it.'

'That's where you're wrong, old man. It'll be you who –'

At that exact moment, the rishi lunged forward, struck the Pishach's jaw with head and then stomped on his feet. The Pishach, who was twice the old man's height, lost his balance and fell, while the other two remained rooted to the spot, confused by such strength from a seemingly ordinary rishi.

Spears in hand, they moved forward, but the rishi deflected their attacks with the staff. While he blocked blows from one Pishach, the other directed his attack towards the woman and children clutching each other in terror.

Clenching his jaw, Nara broke into a sprint, his golden mane flowing around him, his claws shining in the embrace of the sun as he reached the Pishach and sliced through his torso with his nails, tearing his skin and the tendons apart, letting his guts spill out.

The children and the woman cried in horror, hiding their faces from the gore as the Pishach fell on the ground motionlessly. By then, the rishi had handled the other Pishach and knocked him down. Then he turned to Nara. Using his staff to point, he asked, 'Who are you? Are you one of them?' his striking blue eyes flashing.

'No,' Nara said. 'I'm not the enemy here.'

The rishi blinked, realizing his mistake and lowered the staff. 'I … I'm sorry. You just saved my family.' He joined his hands and bowed. 'Thank you, Simha.'

'It's Nara. Narasimha,' he said.

The rishi looked at their saviour. The golden mane of a lion rested on top of his head. He wore the skin of the king of the jungle like an armour over himself. He had a bronze chiselled body with a handsome, defined face.

'I'm Guru Bharadvaj,' the old man bowed again. 'Susheela, take the children inside.'

The woman grabbed the children at once and left, using her hand to turn their gazes from the corpses.

'Let me help you bury them,' Nara said.

The rishi narrowed his eyes in suspicion before nodding. 'Thank you.'

Once they were done, Nara and Guru Bharadvaj performed the Antyeshti, the last rites before leaving the burial site. As they strolled back to the hermitage, Nara asked Bharadvaj, 'Why did they attack a rishi? Isn't that against the laws?'

'We live in a lawless country now, my friend,' the rishi said. He was shorter than Nara, but was fast and agile, and nothing except for his white hair indicated his age. 'They don't care about anything. I left the city to live here in peace, away from their sins, but they still came following me. For what? For saving a life?'

'The bird man,' Nara recalled. 'Who is he?'

'I don't know myself. They were mistaken about the bird man.'

Nara nodded, though there was something not quite right about the way Bharadvaj said it. *Should I believe him?* As a Simha who had been in countless wars and seen many betrayals, it was easy for him to guess when someone was lying. And Bharadvaj certainly seemed to be hiding something.

'Do you want to stay, Lord Narasimha, for some supper?'

'I …' Nara hesitated, but he *was* starving. His stomach growled at the thought of a meal. 'I am off to Kashyapuri actually.'

'Indra's servant in the land of demons? Hmm, that's not going to be taken well. You must properly disguise yourself,' Bharadvaj said.

Nara nodded. He had thought about it. He would wear a shawl around his head to conceal his bronzed features and mane. 'I'm no one's servant. My kin were, but I'm a free man.'

'So you say.'

'But thank you, I'll, uh … stay for some food. I am famished.' Nara sighed, hoping the sound of his stomach growling wasn't louder than the words he had just spoken.

They began to walk towards the huts in silence. As they neared, his nose picked up a scent. Bharadvaj was certainly lying. He could smell a wounded man hidden somewhere on the rishi's patch of land.

2
HIRANYAKASHYAP

He wanted to choke the life out of them. Slowly.

It was all he could think of as he rode alone in the dark, his chest heaving. Behind him, he could see his men following him, but not too close. This was his fight, and his alone.

He halted his horse, and his Brahmshastra, a large golden blade and a thick breastplate, shimmered under the moonlight. It felt so fluid and soft over his body, and it seemed as if it had embraced him tightly. He looked at his men and at Holika on her horse, her twin swords sheathed on her back. A triumphant smile was spreading across her face.

Hiranya nodded to himself as he looked ahead. There was the house, a brick building standing in the lanes of his city. This was where everything had been sabotaged. This was where members of the Vishnusena had been last seen.

Hiranya had been told about this location by his spies, and he was here to destroy them and free his son, Prahlad. The boy who had opposed him, and then abandoned him.

After Anuhrad's death, he had hoped that at least Prahlad would remain under his control, but he hadn't. He had simply vanished. *I'm coming for you, son. And I will save you from being brainwashed any further.*

Hiranya dismounted from his stallion, the sound of his feet creating a metallic thud. He summoned his sword, and it began to form in his hand out of nothing but grey smoke and thin air. It gained shape, a majestic weapon heavy in his hand, a long blade with a golden hilt.

After killing Agni and leaving Yakshlok, he had returned to Kashyapuri only to learn about his sons – one dead, another escaped to be with his enemies. He also heard how Holika had tried to imprison and kill Prahlad, and that had angered him. Even though he understood why she'd done it, he still hated it. Unlike her, he was hopeful. He believed Prahlad could still change. Perhaps he believed that because he was afraid of losing the only chance at posterity he had.

It's over now.

Hiranya sprinted towards the house, the metallic gauntlets on his arm making a clanking sound. He saw two men stationed right outside, looking at him from the shadows. They were the lookouts, going about their business, and when they saw the majestic king of their city coming towards them, they turned tail and began to run.

But Hiranya didn't let them get far. He swung his blade towards one man, slicing him from the torso to his groin, then he sprung at the other, jumping on to his back, and cracked his spine in two. He grabbed the injured man's throat from the back and ripped it out of his body. The lookouts wouldn't be looking out so much any more.

Wiping the blood off himself, he pulled his blade out of the corpse and came to the door of the house. Instead of breaking it down, he knocked.

For a while there was no response. Finally, it opened only a little, almost meekly.

A woman stood there, looking scared when she saw Hiranya's gleaming face – his dark irises and his thin, twirled-up moustache.

Hiranya peered past her into the room and saw that there were a few more unarmed men and women, even children. They all were staring at him, surprised by the new visitor. No one had told them about any intruders! All the lookouts were dead, killed by Hiranya's men who followed behind him.

He looked at the woman in the doorway, and their eyes met in a cold, absolute silence. They both knew blood was going to be shed.

Hiranya walked across the corpses of women, children and men, people who had used this house, inside his capital, and who had festered like rodents. He had slashed all of them. From their torsos to their necks to their limbs. They all lay dead. The walls were burnt to the ground. His men torched the place as he looked around for any sign of life.

'Didn't find anything, I suppose?' a voice chided.

Hiranya turned to see Holika walking up to him. 'No.'

'You didn't have to kill the women and children.'

'They were infected by the idea of someone saving them.' He looked up to the heavens, from where they thought Lord Vishnu would descend to help them. 'They had to realize, at the end of their lives, that not even Vishnu can save them from me.' He glanced at Holika; he could make out a kernel of fear in her eyes.

That fear had sprouted from the capacity for terror and bloodshed that Hiranya displayed from the moment he had received the armour and the blade. He'd known since then that he was omnipotent – he'd known he was a god. And no one could kill a god.

A guard walked up to them, a stack of papers in his hand. 'I believe these are important, my lord,' he coughed, the smoke from the fires still in his throat.

Hiranya took it in his hands. It was a journal, and the name across the top was 'Prahlad'.

'Interesting. I didn't know my son wrote a journal.'

Well, my son is full of surprises.

'Read them,' he thrust the papers at Holika. 'Let me know if you find anything about his whereabouts from this.'

The heat was growing unbearable as the fires were catching on.

'We should leave,' Holika suggested.

But suddenly, there was a loud wail. It came from a cupboard that was slowly being licked by the flames. 'You leave,' Hiranya said. 'I'll join you soon.'

'You'll get burnt!'

'I won't,' Hiranya said. 'I'm invincible.'

Holika grunted and left with the papers and the remaining men.

The king of the Asuras walked to the cupboard from where he could hear the sound of choking. He opened it and saw a young lass hiding inside, whimpering in terror.

Hiranya smiled menacingly. 'It's all right, child. Come out – I won't hurt you.'

She didn't move.

'I will not hurt you, little one, if you tell me where Prahlad and the rest of your men are.'

'I don't know,' she cried out. 'I…I don't know. Prahlad was rescued, and then they left this place. We were also supposed to – you know … we were also leaving soon, but you found us before that,' she coughed. 'We are merely civilians, who believe in the cause. We are not the same as them – the soldiers, who are hiding in a camp. I don't know, I swear … I don't know where the camp is.'

Hiranya nodded as he grabbed her hair and pulled her out of the cupboard. She shrieked in pain and hit him on the chest. The blow bounced off the Asura but left the girl with splintered bones in her hands. He yanked her out, holding her by the throat, lifting her up, as the fires engulfed the remnants of the Vishnusena's hideout.

'Anything else?'

'Erm … ugh …' she choked, clawing at Hiranya's gauntlet, trying to free herself, but she couldn't. She was close to dying. Very close.

And Hiranya was enjoying it. He liked that the last breath of this human was in his hands. He counted the breaths she had remaining as he began to choke her a little harder. And a little more. Until her throat couldn't withstand the force any more, and her eyes slowly drooped before experiencing the sharp snap.

For the first time that evening, he was happy. He had choked the life out of at least one of them.

3

NARASIMHA

As they ate in silence, Nara couldn't forget what he had smelled earlier. Although it was none of his business, he was curious. It intrigued him that a rishi would hide a fugitive. And this bird man the Pishach had referred to. Was it who he thought it was?

Nara applied himself to his plate, eating the mashed vegetables with his hand, while Bharadvaj sat on the ground opposite him, next to his wife and his two children, who were all quiet.

'You are a warrior,' Bharadvaj remarked. 'You have many scars and yet, they are all stitched well.'

'I'm a physician too,' Nara responded.

'A man who both destroys and heals? Interesting!' the rishi exclaimed. 'What other wonders do you have in store for us?'

Nara chuckled. 'Nothing else.'

Bharadvaj looked up and then glanced at his family. 'We shouldn't speak of the intruders – it frightens them.'

11

'All right,' Nara said. 'Are you a physician yourself?'

'Yes.' Bharadvaj nodded. 'I try to make new discoveries in medicine. I have my own clinic, and I primarily work for the well-being of wounded and bruised travellers.'

'That's a noble pursuit.'

'It is, yes.'

'Is it sustainable?'

'We have no need for lavishness – our needs are simple,' the rishi replied.

Nara nodded. He sighed mentally. The journey from the north to the south was tedious, taking many, many days. He had not met many people on the road, but the one time he'd managed to rest was in front of this man, who had a secret. A secret involving someone that Nara might know.

'I began this life,' Bharadvaj said, 'when I was much younger. I saw an Apsara running away from her owners, and she was wounded. I didn't know who she was when I found her. I helped her with whatever little knowledge I had of medicine, and when she was better, she taught me what she knew about shamanic practices. I hope to take that knowledge to the world.'

'Who was this Apsara?'

'Oh,' the rishi sighed, 'that is of no importance. But tell me, Lord Narasimha, do you believe that kindness will always be reciprocated?'

Nara clenched his teeth. His life had taught him the opposite. 'I believe it is. But I also believe that not everything in this world can be solved with kindness.'

'That is unfortunate,' Bharadvaj responded.

'I need to wash my hands,' Nara said, getting up.

'The water jar is outside.'

Nara nodded and stepped out of the dimly lit hut. The wounded man's presence wafted in the air. He knelt close to the jars on the side of the hut, washed his hands and rinsed his mouth before making his way towards the smell.

I have to find out.

He looked back, hoping Bharadvaj had not noticed him walking away. The other hut was completely dark. He tried to pry the door open, but it was shut tight, so he bore down on it with all his might and wrenched it open. He was assailed by the pungent smell of Ayurvedic ointments and festering wounds.

I feel like such an intruder.

Nara wanted to see the wounded man. He walked towards the body on the ground, encircled by lavender-scented candles. The figure had a tall, broad physique with handsome features. His skin was bronze, and on his side lay a mask in the shape of an eagle's head.

It is him. I was right.

He was brutally wounded, and the medicine Bharadvaj had given him was all that held death at bay.

'You shouldn't have come here,' said Bharadvaj from behind him.

Nara turned to see the sage blocking the entrance, his shoulders hunched, hands behind his back. He casually walked up to Nara.

'I know him.'

'You do?' There was mild surprise in his tone. 'I found him and his machine in the woods, both completely broken down. I took him in, and that's why I was attacked by the royal guards. Apparently, he's a fugitive. But to a doctor like me, he's a patient.'

'What has happened to him?'

'He has been poisoned by cordyceps.' Bharadvaj pointed at the purple blotch on the injured man's ribs. 'Shot by an arrow, I presume, which has caused his organs to fail slowly. I have cleaned the wounds and applied some ointments, but the poison remains.'

Nara checked the ribs from afar. He dared not touch the wound, lest it infect him. 'I could perhaps lend a hand in healing him. At the very least, I could help stabilize him until he's fit to stand up, and then find the antidote.'

'I wouldn't mind some help, though you should perhaps ask before you barge into someone else's clinic?'

Nara was immediately apologetic. 'When I heard the Pishach ask about the "bird man", I realized I might know who they were talking about.'

'Who is he?'

'He used to be my best friend,' Nara said. 'His name is Garuda, chief of the Suparns.'

4

HIRANYAKASHYAP

It was the day after he had burned down the Vishnusena hideout. He sat on his throne in the empty halls of his palace.

Hiranya's armour had vaporized for now, and his body felt incomplete – as if he were naked. But he couldn't wear the armour all the time, and especially not just then, for it was twilight, and he couldn't summon it at that hour. Nor could he summon it when he was not on the ground or in the sky. And not when he was inside or outside. These were the rules governing the invincible armour as stated by its creator, Lord Brahma.

Dawn shimmered from the mosaic windows of the palace, casting its pale shadows on the ornate, regal pillars that supported the immense structure. The ground was carpeted with golden sheets woven with red lace. There were lit torches on metal shafts at each end of the carpet. Everything was golden here and yet, he felt there was so much darkness in this room.

He had sent away all his guards. He wanted to be alone, and he wanted to be quiet. His heart ached for Prahlad, Anuhrad and Kayadhu. They were his family – and they were all gone. He was alone with his only remaining sister, who did not always understand him.

'How long do you plan to mope?' a voice echoed in the halls.

Here she comes.

Hiranya looked up to find Holika walking towards him.

Two men followed her closely. Amarka and Shand. Amarka was a thin, lanky man, the minister of cultural affairs, and Shand was the most important man in this city, the treasurer, the minister of finance. He had a bulbous head, and he was short in stature with rough, thinning hair.

'Leave me be,' Hiranya bellowed.

'We have received reports, my lord,' Amarka began. 'Something sinister is outside the gates. The lookouts were supposed to report to us every quarter of an hour, and they have not. That is not normal. We feel an attack upon the city is imminent.'

'By whom?'

'By the very man you have been fighting for so long,' Shand replied. 'We need to strengthen our armoury and prepare our soldiers for any surprises.'

'What about the soldiers on the outer frontier?' Hiranya asked, referring to the guards protecting the gates of Kashyapuri. 'Have they seen anyone?'

'No one so far,' Holika snapped. 'But the lookout hasn't arrived. Something's fishy here.'

'Bah!' Hiranya stood up, grunting under his breath. 'It's nothing. He must have stopped to piss and asked himself what the hell he was doing, serving this kingdom of ashes.'

Holika shrugged. 'I can understand you are hurt at losing your sons, but we have to be prepared for any kind of attack. The battleground on the outskirts of the city, where we have been fighting the Devas, is filled with carcasses for vultures to feed on. The enemy has been quiet for a while. I believe they are planning something.'

'Then stop them.' Hiranya leaned back, bored, until he realized he had something more important on his mind. 'Have you got the report about Prahlad? Have the spies said anything?'

'No.' Holika shook her head. 'The Vishnusena have hidden their new encampment very well, but that should not be our priority.'

'You can't tell the king what his priorities should be. The king decides that.' Hiranya came to his feet, walking from his throne to his sister. 'I don't think you want to find my son – since you were so eager to kill him in the first place.'

Holika flinched, her eyes boring into her brother's. 'He deserved it.'

'I don't care. Have you read the journal?'

'No,' Holika said. 'Because saving this city is more important to me than saving your spoilt son who has betrayed the beliefs we stand for.'

Hiranya clenched his jaw. 'If you were not my kin, I would have killed you with my own hands and let your blood trickle through my fingers.'

He could see the fear in her eyes, though she did her best not to show it. That was his sister – even in the face of death, she would never show her weakness. That was what she had learnt from their guru who trained them back in Pataala.

'This is not the time to fight between ourselves,' Shand intervened. 'We have bigger matters to deal with right now.'

Hiranya shot a look at his minister. 'Tell the spies to double their search parties and find my son. All right?'

'You do realize we need the manpower to take Naglok, just like you took Yakshlok?' Holika said through gritted teeth. 'We can't waste it on a pathetic group of extremists. We are rid of most of them for now.'

'Naglok …' Hiranya turned away, thinking about the stronghold he was yet to conquer. It was the kingdom of the seas, made up of large buildings and beautiful islands. Everyone travelled there on ships, and none would swim, for they would die. It was a city in the midst of an ocean. It was where Varuna was, the Asura who had left and joined Devas. Hiranya hated him. Anyone who could go against his kind was …

He was being a hypocrite, he knew, for he didn't hold the same views for his son. But his son was impressionable, and he could have been easily brainwashed. Hiranya knew he could show him the right path once he got hold of him.

Varuna, on the other hand, was the one who used the strange metal that he mined from the bedrock of the ocean of Naglok and created weapons for the army of the Devas. If the city was taken, the entire armoury of the Devas would be shut down.

But moreover, it held the largest reservoir for their mineral somas or somras – or amrit as it was called by the Devas. They drank it for longevity and power – it was an elixir made for the gods.

And while Hiranya did have a thousand ships to take on this quest, he was more concerned about his son.

'You have the Brahmshastra. It's so powerful, so strong …' Holika said. 'You must not delay.'

'I–I …' Hiranya was conflicted between being a father and a king.

He was distracted from his thoughts by a sudden sound – of crackling, bubbling energy. The bells began to ring, and he knew what they meant.

Hiranya and his group shared a glance before they rushed outside. In the dying light of dawn, the dark skies rumbled as humongous grey elephants with metal tusks broke through the gates and entered his city.

He could see the flags on top of the elephants. He could see his people running for their city. He could hear the thunder in the skies, and he could see his fallibility as a ruler.

With the Simhas on top of the elephants attacking the guards who were in their way, Hiranya realized that it had happened. What Holika had predicted was taking place. And he had stood aside and let it happen.

'Let's go! Summon the Brahmshastra!' Holika cried, before sprinting for the main city where the battle was taking place.

Hiranya remained there, frozen. He looked at the sky: twilight lingered like a dagger over his head. He couldn't summon the Brahmshastra.

What will I do?

5

NARASIMHA

'Hold him – it might wake him up a little,' said Bharadvaj.

Nara grabbed Garuda by the shoulders and held him tightly while Bharadvaj tried to clean his wounds as well as he could.

'I need to remove the poison,' he said, 'but it's a weird one … the poison smells different than most cases I've dealt with.'

'Be careful,' Nara said.

'Tell me, Nara, how do you know him?'

'We served together under Indra a long time ago,' Nara said, tightening his grip as Garuda began to flinch. 'The Suparns are the other half of the Nagas, and not their enemies as is popularly believed. Garuda's mother, Queen Vanita, shared her throne with a Naga queen. Vanita was, uh, a Suparn, an eagle worshipper, and that's why he wears his mask,' Nara said, pointing to the beak-like face mask on the side.

'The eagles and snakes lived together peacefully until the Devas came and complicated matters – like they always do. Initially, they put a minister in Naglok, Varuna, under whom Garuda and his men flourished. He worked under Indra for a while, and thus, worked with me. But the Devas soon turned on them and began to impose harsh restrictions on their way of life. The worst was when they decreed that the reserves of Soma were not to be handed over to the Suparns, who used the elixir to fuel their flying machines.

'The Suparns knew that the Devas were afraid of their machinery. They believed it would make the Suparns stronger than them. Garuda was angry, sure. He and Queen Vanita opposed the Devas, but the Naga queen didn't, causing friction and subsequent rebellions, and finally giving rise to the infamous rivalry between the snakes and eagles. The rest ...' Nara paused, seeing Garuda lying there, ' ... is history.'

Bharadvaj quietly worked on the Suparn chief. In the silence that followed Nara could see that Garuda had begun to flinch and move due to the pain, murmuring under his breath and shaking harshly.

'It's almost done. He's begun to respond to the medicine.'

'Calm him down.'

'Feed him this,' Bharadvaj said, handing Nara a potion in a brass bowl. 'It'll numb him and make him sleep while I finish working on him.'

Nara held Garuda down with one hand, and with the other, tried to slip the potion inside his mouth, but the Suparn chief only grew more agitated as the potion bubbled out of his mouth.

'He's becoming unstable!' Nara exclaimed.

'Hold him tightly!'

Nara grabbed Garuda by the chest and covered his mouth. Garuda opened his eyes, his irises bloodshot, and bit Nara's hand with his infected saliva in his confusion.

Shocked, Nara left Garuda to deal with Bharadvaj's medicines while he wiped off the saliva that stung his skin. Within a second, Garuda's body stopped moving.

'What was that about?' Nara asked. 'And ...' He stopped, feeling his skin growing warm. 'Was he suffering from some kind of fever?'

'I think he's transferred the infection to you.'

Nara fell back against the wall. 'But wasn't it poison?'

'Communicable poison.' Bharadvaj came close to Nara's palm and saw the strands of saliva entering the wound. 'Yes, the infection has been transferred to you. I should have never allowed you in here.'

'*Communicable* poison?' Nara could feel the sweat beading on his forehead, and his body growing weak. 'I have never heard of this kind of ...'

'I know, but you need to trust me. Here, drink this.' Bharadvaj made him drink the same potion that was given to Garuda, to calm his nerves. 'You are both infected now. Just lie still – you'll be fine ... for now.' The rishi's 'for now' sounded quite dangerous.

As Bharadvaj went back to Garuda to stabilize him, a horror-stricken Nara realized he was growing weak.

No, I can't die! I can't die before I meet Prahlad.

And before he could close his eyes to rest, Nara heard Bharadvaj's incredulous voice, 'He's awake! He's awake!'

6
HIRANYAKASHYAP

The king of the Asuras didn't stay frozen for long. He began to run. Without a weapon. Without his armour. He dashed into the thick of battle. There were only three minutes for twilight to break.

Two roaring elephants smashed their trunks against buildings, scattering debris everywhere while their heavy tread created thunderous quakes.

Hiranya's men fought the ravenous Simhas who jumped on every single one of them. He could see Holika on the other side, fighting hand-to-hand with a Simha, using her twin blades.

Hiranya went close to a soldier and snatched his sword and flung it at a Simha. It pierced the eye of the lion-worshipping tribal as he fell down.

Two more minutes to go.

As he battled his way towards the violent elephants, someone grabbed him from behind and pushed him back.

Turning, Hiranya saw it was a Simha. *One of their kind will be my doom*, he thought, recalling Lord Brahma's warning to him.

The Simha began to attack Hiranya, who kicked him in the gut and put all the force in his seven-foot, heavily muscled frame, to punch him full in the face. The Simha recoiled sharply and scampered away. He walked away from the Simha as The cries of wounded civilians, the clashing and the clanging of the metal swords and claws, the zapping energies of bows and arrows and the swish of the beastly trunks had all merged into one.

Hiranya grabbed the nearest weapon from a fallen soldier. It was a javelin.

When the Simha attacked him again, Hiranya turned and, keeping the javelin horizontal, pierced him through and through. Hiranya felt the blood of his enemy splatter his face before he tossed him to the side.

One minute to go.

'MY SON!' came a wail from nearby.

Hiranya stumbled on his feet as he saw a child, confused and lost, about to be the victim of a giant elephant's feet. His mother was being held back by other civilians who seemed to have given up on the child's survival.

Hiranya sprinted forward, his lungs slamming against his chest.

Thirty seconds.

The elephant was almost upon the child.

Twenty seconds.

Hiranya surged ahead, ignoring the other Simhas and the men who were fighting for him.

Ten seconds.

Even as the rampaging elephant lowered its foot, intent on crushing the child underneath, Hiranya barged in, stopping the animal with his massive arms. He invoked Lord Brahma, and his armour immediately manifested itself on his body, shimmering like a golden star.

Face my wrath.

He gave a mighty shove. The huge elephant's strength failed before the awesome power of Hiranya, and the it tumultuously crashed on to the battleground.

The boy was instantly rescued by his mother, who stammered out her gratitude to Hiranya.

'It's nothing. Go save yourselves! Hide!' he exclaimed.

They rushed to do his bidding.

Hiranya pulled out his sword from its golden sheath as he prepared take his enemies down.

As the Simhas began to come at him, darting and moving with speed, Hiranya methodically and clinically slashed through them, one by one, his sword flashing with every turn.

Till, he realized, five Simhas had come around. Circling him.

His armour was streaked with the enemy's blood. Some of it had spattered on his face.

He wiped it.

And smiled.

With every Simha he killed, Hiranya's belief in his immortality strengthened, for Lord Brahma had told him that he could only be defeated by one of their kind. And if he could kill them all, one by one, then there'd be no one left to defeat him …

As his thoughts muddled –

All five Simhas leapt.

Nowhere to hide. Nowhere to run. Hiranya instantly knelt, shielding his face with his arms, while the Simhas tore at his armour with their claws.

For a moment, Hiranya was transported to the loving arms of his mother, who had died too early. He missed her. He missed his father, who wasn't so cruel to him unlike other Asura patriarchs. And he missed his Guruji with whom he practiced a lot during his days in Pataal…

All of a sudden, a fire blazed in his eyes and energy crackled through his body. His armour lit up. He flexed his muscles and heaved upwards, flinging the Simhas off him. Before they could gather their wits and regroup, he grabbed one of them, stabbed him multiple times and tossed the body to the ground. With lightning-fast reflexes he dodged another attack, punched the Simha in the face and beat him to a pulp. He slammed a third into the ground, crushing his ribs. Two Simhas came at him together. Hiranya grasped their necks, but before he could dispatch them, one of them scratched his face. He released them with a growl. Instead of attacking them, he slammed his fist into the earth. The battlefield shook; the Simhas toppled to the ground. With a quick flick of his sword, he plunged it into one's chest and crushed the other's skull with his mighty foot.

Head bowed, he knelt amongst the corpses of some of Indra's finest warriors.

And then he heard the roar. More of them coming towards him.

He stood up, and flexed his shoulders.

Let's do this.

The Simha's severed head fell to the ground.

Hiranya didn't spare a single one of them. After he had taken control of the battle, the remaining Simhas, who should have been taken prisoners of war, were made to kneel before him, all in a line, their hands tied behind their backs, their manes dampened by their own blood.

They were in the centre of the city, on a street littered of a chaotic street, densely populated with the corpses of both his men and Indra's men. Blood was spilled. Guts were scattered.

His remaining warriors stood quietly to the side, all but Holika who dogged his steps as he walked before the Simha soldiers.

'It was said you would be my end, that your kind would hurt me,' Hiranya said through gritted teeth. 'But I believe that to be untrue. I will kill all of you. One by one. If there is no Simha left, there will be no one to hurt me.' He swung his long bluish blade and another head rolled.

'You shouldn't have entered my city. Ordinarily, I would have let one of you go back to your camp and warn them of our triumph, but right now, your deaths will serve as a much bigger warning.' He grabbed another Simha's mane and slashed his throat. 'What a lovely day it is today.'

There were a dozen more Simhas left as Hiranya turned to his men. 'Make sure you torture and then impale them. Display their corpses right outside my lawn for our people to see that nothing can harm us.'

The guards nodded, taking the rest of the prisoners away.

Hiranya sheathed his sword and sighed. He had lost men, and some civilians too. He felt remorse, but more than that, he felt anger.

He looked at Holika, who was staring at him with an expression that said, *I told you this would happen.*

'Find my son,' he ordered her, his eyes blazing. 'I'm leaving.' And with that, he strode back towards his palace.

'Where are you going?' asked Holika loudly.

Without turning, Hiranyakashyap said: 'Naglok.'

7

NARASIMHA

Lying on the patient's bed now, Nara felt that time had fallen into a loop. He blinked, staring at the ceiling as he felt the energy he had lost entering and surging inside his veins again. It was perhaps the ointment or the mashed food Bharadvaj had given him which had brought him back to his senses.

'You are infected as well,' the rishi had said truthfully, standing beside him and grunting under his breath. 'And it's bad. Over the next couple of days, you will experience fatigue, dizziness and paralysis – if I don't find the cure for this poison. Good heavens, you haven't been wounded like Garuda who had to be treated. So, you can still sustain yourself till you find the cure.'

Nara knew the rishi wasn't happy. 'I am sorry. I should have never interrupted your procedure. I was being stupid.'

Bharadvaj frowned. 'Well, we all do stupid things from time to time. Remember that Apsara I told you about?'

'Yes?'

'Well, she was not just my teacher, but my lover.' He paused and then broke into a chortle. 'Don't judge, I was young.'

Nara raised his brows. 'Well, erm...' he didn't know how to feel about knowing a rishi's personal life, but he couldn't help but grin.

Even Bharadvaj chuckled. 'Just thought this anecdote would end some of your worry,' the rishi said with a comfortable smile, as he inched closer to Nara. 'Be careful, Lord Narasimha. You are infected and you have to be cautious and take care of yourself. And do visit me if you have anything you need from me in the future.'

Nara smiled.

And with this, Bharadvaj left him alone.

'How the stars conspire to help us meet, my friend,' a familiar voice said.

Slowly, Nara turned his head to see Garuda leaning against the wall in a golden loincloth, a charming toothy smile on his broad features.

'Hello Garuda,' Nara sighed, sitting up slowly. 'It's been a while.'

'Years, perhaps. Heard you'd given up everything. That makes me wonder what you are doing here,' Garuda said, with a disarming grin.

'Well, you can keep wondering.'

'Always the mysterious lad, eh?' Garuda walked around Nara, eyeing him.

Nara returned his old friend's assessing look. Garuda was somewhat paler than before but still in possession of that familiar winning smile and the mischievous glint in his eyes that glimmered in the room. 'Well, I've just been poisoned. Forgive me if I'm a little grumpy.'

'That would be me, eh.' Garuda touched the bandages on his torso. 'Feels like shit.'

'I know. What were you doing, crashed in the middle of the woods here, so far away from Naglok?'

Garuda scratched his nose. 'Well, after the Nagas betrayed the Suparns by siding with the Devas, I gathered my people into a coup and staged countless revolts against them, stealing the amrit that powers our vimanas bit by bit. But unfortunately, the last revolt failed miserably: several of my men died, our camp was infiltrated, and my mother was captured and taken to that horrible city. I escaped in the nick of time, but I got this bloody arrow in my gut and that's how we find ourselves here, meeting old friends. How destiny creates bridges for us, aye?'

Nara nodded. The story made sense.

'What are you doing here, lad?'

'Well …' Nara narrated his story about how he was part of Indra's battalion before leaving the violence behind and becoming a physician in a village. He was called back to the war to fight against Andhaka and he had managed to kill him. He left out the part about trying to help Prahlad, for that was his personal quest. 'Now I'm just a wanderer.'

'Aren't we all? Well, here's a piece of news for you. This poison that holds us both down can be cured by only one thing.'

'What?'

'You know.'

Nara grit his teeth. 'Amrit.'

'That's right! And you can find a lot of it back in my town,' Garuda said, crossing his arms. 'Though it'll be hard to get since I am a fugitive in that state and you ... you are a deserter.'

'Is there no other way?'

'None. This is a mutated version of *cordyceps* and unfortunately, we have less than a week to find the amrit and ingest it to save ourselves,' he said. 'Now, if you want to wander around as you have been doing, you'll need to be alive for that.'

'Are you sure?' Nara was perplexed. Surely, there were other ways. But Garuda was stern and impassive.

'I know my poison and I know the antidotes, my friend. And believe me, when I say this, there is no other antidote. And you know better than most, when there is no antidote to something, then Amrit is the last resort. Pure, unadulterated Amrit.'

Nara did know that. He had lived long enough in this world to see that everything could be solved by Amrit.

'So you're going all the way to the city that hates you just for amrit?'

'Of course not, lad!' Garuda exclaimed, grinning. 'I have to see my mother and help her escape. And I need go back to the secret hideout of the Suparns where the rest of my colleagues are.'

Nara couldn't believe his luck. Naglok was the last place he wanted to go to. But seeing his friend had brought back a flood of warm memories – of shared meals and laughter, of fighting side by side. Garuda, although an unpredictable ally, had always been there, ready to strike and help Nara whenever the need arose. He didn't really have a choice. It was his own carelessness that had landed him in this predicament. He could try to find another way to cure himself, but that would be risky. He didn't know much of the poison as much as Garuda did … clearly. And who knew how long it would take. The world was an unfair, unpredictable place. *Might as well, get used to it.*

Nara nodded. 'Fine, I'll go with you – not that I have much of a choice.'

'Yes, you don't. There's a merchant vessel I inquired about while you were getting your beauty sleep. It leaves in an hour.'

'Now?'

'Then when?' Garuda chuckled. 'Do you want to start your search for Amrit when you are close to death? Be my guest then. I'm leaving.'

'Fine, fine.' Nara struggled to stand up, since he was feeling weak.

'Hurry up, old man. By the gods of the sky, you haven't changed one bit.'

Nara grimaced at his friend as he clasped Garuda's outstretched hand. Garuda pulled him up.

'Great, I'll get you a cane to walk now.'

I have to listen to these snarky comments for the next couple of days now.

'Okay, I'll get my stuff,' Nara said as he came to his feet. He had to meet Prahlad. Save him from his father in Kashyapuri. But instead of seeking Hiranyakashyap, he was going away from him. To Naglok. Where there would be no Hiranya.

8

HIRANYAKASHYAP

Hiranyakashyap was in his private chambers, preparing for his journey to Naglok the next day. Picking up the goblet of wine, he walked over the window and looked upon his city, blanketed by night. Kashyapuri was in ruins, most of it at least. This latest attacks from Indra had taken its toll on the city. But the destruction had begun before, when Holika and the giants had attacked Prahlad for defying the rules of Asuras and siding with the enemies.

Prahlad …

The son he hoped would take over from him, after Anuhrad's death. But he was gone. Hiranya recalled the promise he had made to his wife … to not hurt their children. But they were forcing him to …

I don't have a choice. What to do? I wish he would come to his senses.

As Hiranya sipped from the goblet in his hand, there was a knock on the door.

Who has come now? At this time?

When he opened the door, the guard said, 'Your highness, she has come.'

She?

As the guard stepped aside to the let the visitor pass, Hiranya protested. 'It's night. No one is allowed to …'

But the person who entered didn't listen.

She had pale white skin and purple dreadlocks and was twice as tall as Hiranya. Had it been anyone else, Hiranya would have killed them by now.

But this was Matali, the preceptor of the Danavs, who ruled at Hiranyapur – the kingdom Hiranya had built for his giant cousins. And she was furious.

Hiranya hadn't been in touch with his cousins for a while and for good reason. They slowed him down. They were strong, no doubt, but Hiranya wanted agility; swiftness.

'Why are you here? We could have met at the dinner–'

'Don't try to ignore the elephant in the room, Hiranya,' Matali snapped. 'How dare you keep your cousins in the dark! We haven't been informed of your plans. It's just a stroke of luck that I was coming to meet you after the attacks and learnt that you are leaving for Naglok.'

Hiranya sighed, and finished the wine in his goblet in one gulp. 'Well, thank you for coming.'

'Do you not want our help? Or will your ego not let you seek any?'

'I will ask for help when I need it.'

'You are losing …'

'I AM WINNING!' he shouted and quieted his cousin. 'And I will continue to win because I have something that not even the Danavs possess.'

Matali was taken aback by Hiranya's hostility. 'In what way have we wronged you that you're excluding us in this manner?'

'I am aiming for progress, Matali. I am aiming for a brighter, faster future.'

'Let's hope you don't burn your feet with so all that speed,' Matali said dryly.

Hiranya chuckled. He was angry but also delighted to be annoying Matali. 'Now, if there's nothing else, you can leave. If I need your help, which I won't, I'll let you know.'

'Don't bother. We won't come even if you need it. When your corpse is frying under the hot sun and your kingdom is perishing because of you indulged your oversized ego, then we will come. Not to save you or your kingdom, but the Asura name.'

Hiranya chuckled again at her vehemence. *Dying under a hot sun! Hah!* He was too strong to be defeated now. 'Some choice lambs were cut today. Stay for few days and let us honour you with a feast. I don't want my dear cousin to go home angry.'

'I am leaving tonight, Hiranya.' Matali said as she walked out of the chamber.

Hiranya looked at the goblet thoughtfully. If he told Holika about this hostility, she would be livid. Best to not say anything and let her think the Danavs were still on their side.

His immediate course of action was clear: He had to leave for Naglok.

9
PRAHLAD

Sitting in front of a bonfire under the blanket of darkness, Prahlad waited with Dhriti and the rest of the Vishnusena for the man who had offered them his help.

His cousin.

Andhaka had stationed himself fifty yards away from their camp and had sent a messenger to say that he would be coming in his caravan to discuss his plans, plans that would help the Vishnusena.

'We can't trust him,' Prahlad said, turning to Dhriti and the new leader of Vishnusena, Asamanja. 'He is ... a strange one.'

Asamanja had scars all over his body. His waist-length hair and thick, bushy beard were braided like a tribal's. 'I am sure he is, but we really don't have much of a choice right now.'

'He knows our location,' Dhriti cautioned. 'We need to move our campsite.'

'And we will,' Asa said. 'As soon as this meeting is over. I am curious to know what he has in mind.'

Prahlad sighed under his breath. Asamanja had been the favourite candidate to succeed Narada since he was the oldest in the group and had much experience in strategizing and planning. Prahlad had little knowledge about his background – the only thing he knew was that Asamanja's wife had been taken away and raped by the city soldiers, and then left in the gutters. He had tried for a month to find her until he saw her body floating in the sewer, her face chewed off by rats.

The depth of Asa's hatred towards Hiranya's empire was unfathomable. He wanted to hurt those men. He'd never had his revenge, for he didn't know which guards were responsible.

'It's funny though,' Asa said, 'that you don't trust your cousin.'

'I don't trust my family,' Prahlad said emphatically. Dhriti clasped his fingers in her own and gave him a warm, reassuring smile.

'That's very interesting,' Asa replied.

That was when the sound came. Prahlad's blood ran cold. *I hear it!*

The sound of hoofbeats coming nearer by the minute.

Prahlad held his breath as he saw a white stallion emerge from the darkness. The rider was a bald man draped in a red cloth. Behind him, there was ... no one. Andhaka had come without his men. Why? *He knows we can hurt him.*

The horse stopped a short distance from the huge bonfire, and the rider dismounted. Andhaka was as Prahlad remembered him – pale and lanky with long, bony fingers that were caressing the crimson cloth draped over him like a blanket.

'Hmm,' he sighed under his breath, sniffing, as if he was trying to find out the number of men there just by smell.

Asa had put two guards with spears on either side of their large group, ready to strike if something sinister was played out here.

'A hundred and one,' Andhaka said.

'*What*?' Asa replied.

'A hundred and one of you, and you couldn't have chosen a better place to hide, hmmm?' he chuckled.

'How did you …' Asa was both awed and shocked. Before he could give away anything Prahlad put up a hand to silence him.

'It's good to see you, brother,' he said.

For a moment, Andhaka was frozen in place, and then a thin smile crossed his face. 'As my reports suggested, you are indeed here. I didn't believe father's favourite boy would be here. Come, give your brother a hug.'

Prahlad licked his lips thoughtfully when he was nudged by Asa to go forward. Ignoring the worried glance from Dhriti, he strolled towards Andhaka and embraced him. He could smell something off of him right away – ginger and ash.

'You have chosen the right path,' Andhaka whispered in his ear. 'Anuhrad would have wanted you to.'

Prahlad pulled back. 'What do you know about Anuhrad?'

'I was there when he was killed.'

'By whom?' Prahlad clenched his teeth.

Andhaka paused momentarily. Prahlad detected a slight flicker of unease on his cousin's face, before it broke into a grim smile.

'A casualty of war, unfortunately,' he replied, dodging the question.

Prahlad didn't have the energy or the state of mind to speak about Anuhrad right now. The very fact that his brother was dead was not something he was ready to face. He dreamt of Anuhrad often, sweet, nectar-like dreams in which they were together, until suddenly Prahlad would find himself alone. He would wake up in a cold sweat, feeling lost and bereft, tears trickling down his cheeks. Yet he couldn't share his grief with anyone for fear of being thought weak.

Even though he was sure his cousin was being insincere, Prahlad smiled at him weakly.

'It was a grievous loss, brother. I mourn him.'

'Me too. He was a great man.' Andhaka apologetically looked down.

Yes, he was.

Prahlad returned to his place by the fire as Andhaka put his hands behind his back and said: 'Hmmm, perhaps a short introduction is in order. I am Andhaka, the ruler of the Asura empire in the north, but I faked my death and came to you when I learnt Prahlad was here. I came without my men, so you know I mean business and I offer friendship, hmm.' He paused for effect.

The entire Vishnusena was silent.

'Anuhrad, Prahlad's brother, and I were close,' he continued, `but we were both betrayed by the empire, hmm. And now I stand here, with my army, ready to take down the Asuras with you.'

'Why?' Dhriti asked.

Prahlad could tell that Andhaka had an agenda, but he would have to wait to discover what it was.

'When I was a child, my dear girl, I used to be tied to my chair and held against my will in a dark room. I was fed once a day. One day, my late father, Hiranyakshak, brother of Hiranyakashyap, ruler of Kashyapuri – brought me food three times. Oh, I was deeply surprised, but it turned out that the food was poisoned. The kind of poison which makes you spit blood, creates ulcers and makes you so sick that you want to die – but doesn't kill you. My father said he was making me invulnerable to any attempts on my life involving poison.' Andhaka shook his head glumly. 'I was eight years old.'

In the deathly silence that followed, a shiver ran down Prahlad's spine. He had never imagined the cruelties his uncle had inflicted on his son.

'So when I tell you, hmmm, that I have reasons to destroy the Asura empire – I have reasons. I want to annihilate the legacy my late father wanted the Asuras to have, so he can suffer in the afterlife. And to do this, I need people who can help me in this crusade. Believe me when I say this: I am selfish. I am not here to help you. I am here, so that you can help me.'

The Vishnusena was shocked by Andhaka's brutal honesty. Prahlad was concerned for his cousin's mental state. He could not imagine what he must have endured. No matter how cruel Hiranyakashyap was, he wasn't like Andhaka's father.

'How did you find us?' Asa asked, breaking the silence.

'Easy – I pay a lot of travellers for information. They act as my ravens, hmm,' Andhaka said. 'The information I received was that you still have the fire to take down the empire after the debacle in the city. And I know just the way to cripple them.'

'Why do we need you?' Asa chuckled. 'We can do it ourselves, frankly.'

'Sure you can,' Andhaka shrugged, 'but will you do it as well and as thoroughly as you could with me? I can be very useful in a war. Prahlad knows that.'

Prahlad swallowed awkwardly as everyone turned to him for confirmation. He had heard about Andhaka's campaigns against the Devas and other enemies. They were known to be methodical and smart, but he hadn't witnessed any first-hand. But he felt sorry for his cousin after hearing his story, and out of kindness, he said: 'He's right. He was my father's strongest ally. He can be useful, depending on what he proposes as a plan.'

Asa wasn't convinced, but Dhriti locked her fingers with Prahlad and showed her support, even though she herself was a bit unsure.

'Hmmm, thank you brother. Yes. I have a plan. And it's the most obvious, simple plan. Take away the money. The government is crippled, the army stops supporting them, and there will be no soldiers to defend the gates. How does that sound?'

Everyone in the Vishnusena began to murmur, but Prahlad was not surprised. Andhaka's plan made sense. The idea of breaking into the treasury seemed daunting, but there was a fire in him now, a lot of anger. There was no conflict in the way he used to live. There was pure hatred towards his father, his empire and his men.

'It sounds outlandish,' Asa said, giving voice to Prahlad's concerns. 'I tell you, we should just blow the bloody gates.'

'In all fairness, Chief, you don't have the manpower to do it,' Andhaka said, and there were a few chuckles.

'So what do you suggest?' retorted Asa. 'How do we cripple them? We don't know anything about the treasury. Where is it located? Do you know?' he turned to Prahlad who shook his head in response, feeling useless. 'Great. Even the son of the king doesn't know, so who will?'

Andhaka smiled. 'Well, there is one person who can get us accurate information, but we need to capture him quietly.'

'Who?' Prahlad asked.

Andhaka smiled. ' The minister of finance – Shand. The last I knew, he was still in Kashyapuri. He will tell us everything about looting the city if we get to him.'

'How much can you really vouch for him?' Asa asked sceptically as some of the senior members of the Vishnusena looked on, clearly sharing their leader's doubts.

They were in a dark room, lit by a few candles. Asa and the others had cornered Prahlad immediately after Andhaka had left for his camp. Dhriti was the only one on his side. Always. Never leaving him.

'I don't know him enough. I met him when I was young…'

Asa grunted. 'You told there that he was–'

'He is good,' Prahlad interrupted in a soothing tone, hoping to make them understand. 'My father was a great fan of his strategies. We should give him a chance. Let's see what he comes up with. It's not like we have anything to lose.'

'What if he tells your father about our location?'

'If he had to,' Dhriti intervened, 'he would have done so by now and we would be a pile of smouldering ash. I think his intentions will work in our favour.'

Asa stared at Prahlad, still uncertain.

'Chief,' Prahlad began with grit in his voice, 'if he does something that is in anyway questionable–' he paused to look at the stark, worried faces of the Vishnusena members, then continued – `I will be the first to plunge a dagger in him.'

10

CHENCHEN

'There it is – just be careful.' And then she twisted his neck.

The man groaned in pain, and was immediately flooded by a sense of ease and relief. He grinned. 'Oh god, that feels good!'

Chenchen smiled as she looked at the wounded warrior with the stiff back on her table. She was giving him therapeutic massages to relieve his pain. She moved to his legs and then pulled the left one with methodical precision as his muscles creaked loudly. She then stretched his other leg and his arms as well.

After a battle, soldiers would often experience stiffness, get backaches, and that's where she came in. And even though the defeat of Andhaka had left them with no enemy in the north, there were a few tribals whom they had to still fight.

Seeing the soldier's mane flowing down the side of the table, she missed Nara desperately. She hadn't seen him for many days now, and his absence was a constant ache in her chest. Every time she saw a Simha, her heart would feel heavy at the memory of him.

A few minutes later the soldier got up and left after thanking her profusely. She had turned around to wash her hands in the bowl when she heard someone say softly, 'Hello, miss.'

Chenchen turned to see a tall man with white hair on the sides of his bald head and a loose moustache hanging over his lips. When he entered the room, the skies roared thunderously.

'Lord Indra?' Chenchen whispered under her breath.

She had heard that Lord Indra and his army had entered the fortress that belonged to Lord Shiva after Nara had destroyed the Pashupatastra. But she never thought he would come to meet her.

'How may I be of service, my lord?' She didn't like the man – she had heard truly awful things about him. But when he was standing there in front of her, she just saw a weak, frail man with sunken cheeks and wrinkles crowding his face. But even with all his frailties, he still had a dominating presence in the room.

'I've heard you were close to Nara. That you saved him in a fight by killing his opponent with a crossbow.'

'Yes, I did.'

'Can you then help me understand why he would want to destroy the only weapon which could have saved us?'

'He saw the repercussions that the weapon had on our people,' she said, remembering the time when Narasimha and she had seen the village which had suffered the radiations of the nuclear weapon – Pashupatastra.

Indra gazed at her, but there was no emotion in his eyes. It was just a stare, and one that felt icy. 'I see. How will we manage to end the Asuras' reign now?'

'With a treaty perhaps?'

He shook his head. 'We are in way too deep to propose a treaty now. It would have been great to have had Nara on our side.'

'But I am afraid he doesn't want to. He feels …' and she knew she would spark a fire by saying this, but she was brave enough to do so, 'both sides of the war are the worst kind of humans who are letting innocent people in between die.'

He shot her a curiously blank look. 'I agree. I have beaten myself up over that more times than I care to discuss.' He paused. 'Tell me, why are you here and not with Nara?'

'Because I am where the patients are.'

'Do you know where he went? I would love to talk to him.'

'I don't know,' she lied.

'Ah, all right,' he said, coming forward. 'You treat the sick, isn't it?'

She nodded.

'Then treat Lord Bhairav's wife. Parvati. Ever since I told her, she has gone mad, hoping to find her son.'

'What do you mean?'

'I told her Andhaka was alive,' Indra said. 'One of our soldiers caught sight of him after Nara had defeated him on his land, but he vanished quickly.'

Chenchen's blood ran cold. *But Nara vanquished him.* 'How is he …'

'We can only wonder.' He shook his head. 'Anyway, I have a request. Talk to Lady Parvati and keep an eye on her. I am leaving this place. My son awaits me at Naglok.'

Chenchen didn't acknowledge his request, and he didn't give her time to do it either. He simply left.

Chenchen thought about Parvati. She could understand what the other woman was feeling right now. She would be ecstatic that her insane son was alive.

No. Chenchen realized. *I can't let ...*

As she stood there contemplating what to do, Chenchen heard another knock on the door. 'Come in,' she said.

And they did. In their dozens and dozens. The nurses with their head wraps and their muted colours crowded her room, all looking dazed and unhappy.

'What is it?'

'It's just that ... Madam, we were thinking of leaving,' one of them said. 'After the Andhaka episode, we don't have much purpose here.'

'All of you?'

'Yes.' They nodded together.

'But ...' She wanted to come up with a reason for them to stay, but they were right. There hadn't been a battle for a long time, except for few tribal bandit attacks, and those didn't need a lot of medical attention.

'We want to be useful somewhere,' another nurse said. 'We plan to go to various villages and then move once our jobs are done. Travelling nurses if you will.'

Another one piped up, 'And we want to travel to the east and west and south. The blizzards in the north may be too hard to bear. But what we really want to say is this – we would love it if you would join us.'

The idea seemed good because a lot of villages did need help, but she didn't know whether she should go. She didn't know whether she wanted, even though she had decided that being here was it. Suddenly, the face of Lady Parvati appeared in front of her. Andhaka was alive and if Chenchen wanted to make sure that he didn't become a wreck again, she had to meet Lady Parvati.

'I would have,' she smiled. 'But I have something else that I need to take care of.'

At midnight, she stepped out on the snow. With her fingers laced inside her satin gloves, Chenchen forged ahead, her black hood pulled low over her face as she walked towards Lady Parvati's home. It was bigger than the others in the fort, and as she neared it, she heard the trampling of hooves.

Horses were lined up in front, and Chenchen saw a woman in a purple dress walk around and climb up on one of them. The guards around her were bemused, but the woman didn't seem to care. Her saddle was heavy with weapons of all kind.

Chenchen walked towards her, speaking: 'My lady, what in heaven's …'

Parvati turned and eyed her. 'What are you doing here?'

'I heard about Andhaka.'

Her eyes filled. 'Yes, I heard too.' She told the guards to put the other horses in the stable. Her eyes on the main gate, she said, 'I plan to leave. And I'm glad you are here. I require a medical assistant on my journey, someone who could tend to my wounds if I am hurt.'

'To prevent injury, you have Lord Veerabhadra's soldiers.'

'I don't belong here after Bhairav's death, Chenchen,' she smiled sadly. 'I kept mourning the death of my son and now, when I know that he's alive, I can't sit idle in my house and weep. Will you come with me?'

'To do what?'

'To help him. I want him to realize that his mother loves him, and I hope to change him.'

Chenchen didn't want to leave, but she also knew there were no patients here any more. They didn't really need her, and she didn't like it here without Nara. Perhaps if she went out in the world, she would find him. Perhaps. One could only hope.

'Do you know where he is?' Chenchen asked.

'No.' Parvati smiled. 'But I know someone who might know.'

'Who?'

'The sisterhood I belonged to before my marriage,' Parvati said. 'The Matrikas.'

11

HOLIKA

This is not good. Holika read the scroll she had just received from a guard. 'No, it's not good at all,' she murmured before turning to the guard and asking, 'Are you sure?'

He nodded.

'All right. Call him in – I need to have a word with him,' Holika commanded. The guard bowed and left her office.

She leaned back in her seat, set the scroll on the table and blankly stared at the ceiling. Thoughts about the contents of the scroll swam in her mind, and she wondered how this would now pan out.

Hiranya had departed days ago, leaving her in charge of Kashyapuri. She had strengthened the security, and familiarized herself with every nook and cranny of the city in the wake of the recent attack. The restoration of the city walls was ongoing, there was continuous military involvement in the day-to-day life of the people. The army had strengthened in the outer circle of the city.

She picked up Prahlad's journal and began to flip through it. Most of it was gibberish – musings about his life, his relationships with his father and his brother, and the absence of his mother. A few pages later, she saw her own name and began reading:

'I have never seen my mother except for the portraits my father has in his room. But he had told me if I needed someone to share things with, I could go to my aunt, Holika. But she was always cold, and would sneer at me. She wouldn't talk to me. I never understood why. I was both curious and sad about it, and there were days when I wanted to ask her why she hated me. But I didn't ask her – I asked my brother.

And he told me, 'Stay away from her. She hates us since she can't bear her own children, and despised our mother for having two.' But instead of pushing me away from her, it made me understand her. I wanted to do something nice for her.

So I wrote a poem since I had been learning poetry. But it was all broken and haphazard. Oh dear, it was horrible, and when I think about it now, I blush. But still, like an enthusiastic eight-year-old, I trotted to her door, hoping to give her my flawed words. When she saw me, she simply stared. That stare. It was like ice piercing my soul.

"What do you want, boy?" she rasped.

"Uh, no, nothing," I said, frightened by her presence. All I wanted was to tell her that I had written her a poem, so she would not feel that she had lost the chance to be a mother. That she already had a son. I would even have called her "Mother". But I don't think she ever acknowledged me'.

Holika clenched the papers in her fist, tears brimming in her eyes. She had not expected this. She placed the papers back. If she had been cold to Prahlad, it was from the frustration of not having children of her own, but she should have realized – she did have them. She shook her head, recalling how Simhika, the girl she had called daughter had been killed because of Prahlad. Had she given him the love that a child needs from his mother, would he have turned out different?

Holika was still thinking about it when she heard a knock on the door. *He's here.*

'Come in,' she said.

A man stepped in.

'We seem to have a problem,' Holika said. 'My men say that strange kids have been following you around, checking up on your daily activities. We interrogated one of those kids and found that they were being paid by the Vishnusena to keep track of your movements. Perhaps they want to know what time is suitable to capture you, Shand.'

The fat, bulbous man looked concerned. He took a handkerchief in his hand and wiped the sweat from his forehead. 'Oh dear, my lady, how should I … I won't go out any longer.'

Holika shook her head. 'On the contrary, you should continue going out,' she smiled. 'I have something in mind.'

12

NARASIMHA

'Have you taken off your mane? These are deep waters,' Garuda said. 'And the chances of us getting caught if we don't hide our identities are pretty damn high.'

Nara had already taken his mane off, and it was now carefully wrapped in his hand, that he slung against his chiselled frame. He looked like an ordinary man, as did Garuda who had taken off his Suparn mask.

The vessel suddenly lurched over the choppy waters. The captain, a drunkard, kept serving shots of sura to his crew, getting them drunk as well.

Nara watched the deep trench waters that went beyond the horizon. Even though their ship was in the middle, from here it looked like the entire world was submerged. This was the place most affected by the flood caused by the Asuras during Lord Varaha's time. And while others pushed the waters out of their domain, the Nagas in Naglok embraced it. They made vimanas and advanced ships to travel. They created a kingdom out of this place.

And just like the snow that engulfed the entire north, the west was covered in water.

'Do you remember your mother?' asked Garuda.

'No, Simhas don't remember their parents – they don't even meet them. All they have is their chief and their lion companion.'

'Ah, it's shit to be you, I suppose,' Garuda chuckled. 'My Amma was a great woman, probably the worst type since she was so kind. But the Nagas betrayed her, again and again and again. Horrible, shitty men they are, I tell you. I remember her feeding me soup as a young boy; she always did make the best soup in bloody Illavarti. I tell you, it's not the person you miss; it's the things you associate with them. Soup. Warmth. Something like that. God, if only I could bring her back and ask her to make that soup.'

'You sound selfish.'

'I am not. As much as I don't admit it, I love that old hag.' He cracked his knuckles. 'And now she's bound there, like some dog on a leash.'

'You should have brought backup.'

'And lose my men? I'm better off not drawing too much attention – just sneak in and sneak out. I know the bloody kingdom better than the crevices of my ass.'

'Do you always swear so much or do you save it for me?'

'Well, put cotton in your ears then,' he chuckled. 'I am not going to stop being vulgar. I like my tongue and the words that flow from it.'

Nara remained quiet. Garuda had always been this abrasive, abusive fellow who would kill a man and spit on him just out of spite. He often spoke of his mother, even during his early expeditions with the Devas when Nara had accompanied him. Nara sighed, and turned to go back to his bunker and take a nap. That's when he saw it.

In the distance. Visible under the auroras of the sky.

'What a glamorous beauty it is!' exclaimed Garuda, looking ahead.

And it was. Right in the middle of the abundant ocean, stood Naglok, made of granite and marble, with tall towers and conical structures, arched gates and a lot of ships, both merchant and military. Children ran over the docks as though they were on a playground.

'Look at what the Devas did to this beauty! But not for long.'

'Why?'

Garuda turned. 'You haven't heard? The water is drying and the Devas aren't doing anything about it – the skies haven't favoured us with their tears in a long time. The water is lower than it was before and soon it'll be dry as my Amma's skin. This is karma, I tell you. What you do to the bloody world, the world shits back at you. Treat it well, I say.'

Nara simply nodded.

As the ship sailed closer to Naglok, Nara could see the beaches that surrounded it, acting as ports for other vessels to harbour. Nara came close to the hull and took a deep breath, inhaling the fragrance of seaweed, when he saw another ship nearing them.

'All aboard!' shouted the drunk captain. 'Inspection time.'

As the shadow of the military vessel stretched over their ship, Nara's heart began to race. He glanced at the worried Garuda, who knew this wouldn't end well.

They both walked to the captain while the military ship prepared for boarding.

'What is going on, friend?' asked Garuda. 'This is a merchant vessel. Why are we …'

'Oh, shut up, both of you!' the captain said.

'It was only me speaking, actually,' Garuda replied.

'Well, I heard two voices. Ships are often inspected – without any reason, I believe.'

Garuda pulled Nara to an alcove. From the corner of his eye he saw Nagas officers stepping on the deck of their ship. 'How good a swimmer are you?'

'I can't swim.' Nara said, almost drowning in his fear of water. 'It's probably the only thing that frightens me.'

'Spoken like a true lion,' Garuda muttered sarcastically. 'We need to scram otherwise we will be caught.'

'Why don't we just act normally? I'm sure not every officer in this land knows you.'

'I'll have you know,' Garuda grit his teeth, 'every corner of this kingdom is lined with portraits of me.'

'And yet, you planned to sneak in?'

Garuda wrapped a shawl over his face. 'I thought this would be enough.'

'Wow! I don't recognize you – at all. Where is Garuda?' Nara said with a straight face.

'Rest your funny bones until we …'

An officer approached them from the side. 'Identification?'

The puckered blue eyes of the Naga pinned them both down as Nara pulled out the papers Garuda had given him – fake documents that had been bought from the captain.

The officer read the papers while Garuda, with the shawl over his face, kept looking on the other side.

'Your friend doesn't like to show his face, eh?' asked the Naga soldier.

'Well, he's shy.' Nara grinned. 'Everything okay, officer?'

'Seems fine,' he said and handed back the papers. Garuda smirked behind the corner of his shawl. 'I would like to see your bag too.'

Nara nervously glanced at Garuda. 'Both our bags?'

The officer said, 'Both, yes. Just a quick peek.'

'Um ...'

Nara handed over his bag, and the Naga shuffled through it. He pulled out the mane. 'Ah, a Simha. What a delight. You are a soldier of the empire. What are you doing on a ship like this?'

'Well ...' Nara shrugged, I don't mean to brag, but I'm a writer apart from being a warrior, and I have developed a fascination for the pirates on these shores.'

The Naga soldier grinned. 'Well, a writer, eh? Quite an adventurous hobby.'

'Not as much as you think.'

The soldier handed the bag back to Nara with a smile, who took it with an answering smile.

Safe!

'Yours, sir?' the Naga asked Garuda.

'My friend,' Nara intervened, remembering the signature beak in Garuda's bag which would instantly get him imprisoned, 'is an associate. Since I'm a warrior of the empire, do you think you could let us go? That's the least you can do for us, right?'

The Naga narrowed his gaze suspiciously as Nara waited, sweat beading on his forehead.

'All right!' The Naga grinned. 'As you say, sir. I'll tell Lord Jayant that a Simha is coming to our land.'

'Jayant? He's here?' Garuda whipped around, partially revealing his face.

The Naga arched his brows. 'Hold on a minute – I've seen that face somewhere.'

'No, you haven't,' Nara said.

'Yes, that's right – you haven't,' Garuda added.

'No, no, I have. Remove your shawl, please.'

Nara and Garuda shared another glance.

'You asked for it.' Garuda shook his head and took off his shawl, revealing his face.

'Hey! That's the bloody rebel!'

It wasn't the Nagas who cried out, but some of the other soldiers who had noticed Garuda.

'THE SUPARN!' another other soldier shouted.

'Sorry, my friend, to leave you like this,' Garuda said, shrugging as he punched the Naga in the throat and ran towards the ship's rails to jump off. But before he could escape, Nara and he were surrounded by a dozen armed Nagas.

'Don't move, or we will shoot! And you can't swim forever if you're wounded,' a Naga bellowed, taking aim with his crossbow.

Nara could have fought them, but to what purpose? He was feeling extremely weak since being poisoned; the soldiers would overpower him in moments.

Garuda remained on the railing, frozen, before he stepped down. 'Fine, I'm yours. The Great Flying Man is yours.'

'Do they call you that?' Nara asked.

'Well …' Garuda raised his arms in surrender and so did Nara. 'Jayant does. The bloody heir to Devlok is a pain in the ass, I tell you. And he has my mother locked up. He was the one who sent the army to hurt me, but I didn't know he would still be here. That bloody bunny is always hopping around.'

As the Nagas tied their hands and feet together with thick vines, the drunkard captain stood up and loudly said, as if he was acting on stage: 'HOWWWWW IS THAT POSSIBLE? They also have fake documents in case you need to put some more charges on them.' And he looked at Nara and Garuda with red eyes. 'What a shame, what a shame!'

Nara hated the position he was in. As it is the poisoning had weakened him and delayed his original mission. And now, death seemed imminent. Things were not going well. He couldn't imagine what would happen when Jayant found him, knowing very well that he was a deserter.

13

PRAHLAD

They had to move fast. They had to get in from one door, sneak past the guards, find Shand and threaten him to go leave from the back door. They had already studied the tavern and knew that it opened to a second exit where Shand's guards wouldn't be stationed. That was where their chariot would be waiting.

As a minister, Shand would normally have had more security, but he didn't want to attract attention since he was at a dance bar at midnight and he was, after all, a minister.

Prahlad stood with Dhriti, holding hands. He was scared, since he was the one going in. He had volunteered even though Asamanja had warned him that if anyone recognized him in the city, he would likely die. But he didn't give in to the fear. This was the least he could do for the group that had saved him from certain death.

To enter the main gates was sheer stupidity, but being the former Prince, he knew certain nooks and corners from where they could enter and disappear into busy spaces. If Indra ever got these plans, it would be the end of Kashyapuri. But that is not what they wanted. They wanted the city to soar again, but under more stable leadership than the one it had currently.

Standing under the starry sky, Prahlad saw the tavern in the middle of the empty street. Two guards stood outside, their hands on their sword hilts.

'Are you ready?' he asked Dhriti.

'Oh, I am!'

They both wore hoods with attached capes. 'I hope Asa is waiting for us on the other side.'

'I made sure he is,' she replied.

They began to walk towards to the tavern, and as they neared, their body language changed. They pretended to be a couple of drunks, slurring, hiccupping, staggering on their feet.

'What are these ... what are these ...' Prahlad kept repeating, hiding his face from the guards, who weren't paying attention to the two drunkards until they were at the door.

'Wait,' the guard said, stopping Prahlad. 'Who are you?'

'I am the king of the city, you dummy!'

'Hmm,' he said, pausing for a moment. 'Take off your hoods.'

They had anticipated the order, and they had the perfect response for it. 'No, I won't,' Prahlad drunkenly answered. 'All right, sweetheart?'

'Shut up!' shouted the guard as he pulled the hood away.

Everything happened in a flash. Dhriti pulled her baton out of her cape and smacked one of the guards' rear, simultaneously slamming it down on the other man's toe. Both guards fell to the ground, groaning in pain.

'We have five minutes before they follow us in – hurry!'

As they stepped inside the tavern, they straightened and got ready to find their target.

Prahlad saw the peasants, labourers, crooks, merchants, traders and nobles, all in one place, slouched in on their chairs, sipping wine and ale while they stared at the attraction on the stage in the middle – a naked woman with twenty bangles on each arm, and her hair tied in a loose bun, dancing sultrily.

They began to navigate between the tables and chairs until they caught sight of Shand, sitting casually in a corner, sipping from a goblet. He didn't have a lot of people around him. It looked like a section for important people.

Prahlad and Dhriti walked towards him and took a seat on either side. For a second, he was confused and said: 'This is a private area. I hope you don't think …'

Dhriti brought a blade to his throat. 'Get up and start walking,' she whispered.

Meanwhile Prahlad scanned the crowd and the path to the back door, which they would use as an exit. It was ten yards away across the bar.

Shand chuckled, his face reddening up.

'You think this is a good time to laugh?'

He looked at Prahlad. 'I know it's you, boy. Aren't you ashamed of yourself? Your father weeps for your insolence and your betrayal.'

'Do as the girl says,' Prahlad said.

'I am not doing anything.'

At that moment, Prahlad saw the guards entering the tavern, trying to find them. They were losing time. He exchanged a glance with Dhriti, before he wrapped the garrote he had brought with him for this mission around the minister's fleshy neck and dragged him away from the table, towards the door.

All the patrons began to shout, and overturn tables and chairs in their haste to run away, getting in the guards' way. Prahlad kicked open the door and pulled the fat man across with difficulty.

'What are you doing? HE WILL DIE!' Dhriti screamed.

Prahlad noticed that Shand's face had gone as pink as a peach, and there were tears in his eyes as he coughed uncontrollably. But he didn't care. The chariot was just a few steps away, a small one compared to the ones he used to travel in as a king. Asa was in the front, waiting for them to put Shand in.

Prahlad forced the fat man to enter , then waited while Dhriti followed. He was about to board when the door swung open and the guards rushing out, flustered and angry.

'Go, go!' Prahlad yelled, grabbing hold of the ledge of the chariot as Asa whipped the horse. It neighed before taking off at a fast clip, leaving the chasing guards behind.

Prahlad hung from the side of the carriage, while inside Dhriti kept her blade across Shand's throat. The minister was still gasping, trying to catch his breath after being nearly choked to death.

'I think this was a success!' Prahlad chuckled.

Asa laughed, so did Dhriti, but she leaned close to Prahlad and whispered: 'What got into you?'

'I don't know,' he could only remember feeling a towering rage towards Shand for some inexplicable reason. 'I think ...'

'MY DEAR FRIENDS!' Asa yelled as they heard the sounds of another set of wheels rattling behind them, racing to catch up—as if they knew exactly who was in the chariot. 'We have company.'

'How did they …' Prahlad's face contorted in surprise. 'This is not good.' When he saw who was on the chariot, it got a whole lot worse. It was his aunt.

Holika.

14
HOLIKA

'MOVE FASTER!' Holika yelled at her charioteer, her twin blades gleaming in her grasp, poised to strike.

The man whipped the horses, leading them closer to the rebels. Holika brought out her crossbow and took aim at the other chariot, narrowing her gaze. *Come on. I need to do this.*

She couldn't aim properly for both the chariots were moving too fast – she released the catch, but the arrow went elsewhere. She shot again, and the arrow swooped and struck one of the cloaked kidnappers. There was a loud yelp as the figure's hood fell off, and he turned to look at Holika.

It was Prahlad.

Holika instantly dropped the crossbow. *Prahlad!? I must be careful.*

'Ram into it,' she ordered her man, who nodded and manoeuvred the chariot into hitting the other one on its side. Prahlad's chariot moved a little, but they didn't retaliate. They were focussed on the road, on trying to find a way to escape.

'AGAIN!' Holika commanded.

Her chariot lurched forward, bumping the other one hard as it pulled up alongside. Holika raised her blade to smash the other chariot's wheel so that it would topple, but just then she saw Prahlad's face.

No. If I do that, he might get hurt – maybe even die.

Holika had never cared about anyone during combat. But reading his journal …

Frustrated by the direction her thoughts were taking, she hesitated momentarily. In that split second, she saw Prahlad fling his own blade at her charioteer, striking his throat with excellent precision. The man fell to the side of the chariot, letting the reins go slack in his hands. Holika instantly grabbed the reins and began to whip the horses, urging them to move faster. 'COME ON!' She yelled.

Together, the chariots hurtled through the alleys and the roads, passing and hitting each other, sparks flying as their wheels clashed corrosively.

She dodged the arrows that were being shot at her until …

One arrow crashed into her armour. The impact almost toppled her from the chariot, but she managed to right herself by grabbing on to the side with one hand and the reins with another. To her dismay she saw that Prahlad had gained some ground and widened the gap between them. Hoping to speed up she kicked the charioteer's corpse off the chariot. But his body came under the wheel and it flipped her chariot, causing her to tumble and fall along with her black stallions.

She had hoped to take the enemy by surprise so as to not draw the attention of the public as well as the kidnappers. But she had been arrogant. She had thought she would be enough to take them down. She had been wrong.

The image of her nephew was imprinted in her eyes in the moments before she was claimed by the friendly face of darkness.

15

HIRANYAKASHYAP

'WEAK!' Hiranya called out to his son.

Anuhrad jumped forward and Hiranya again dodged him with ease.

'WEAK!' Hiranya scowled. 'What has gotten into you, boy?'

Gritting his teeth and clenching his fist, his young son charged at him angrily. Hiranya instantly punched him in the face.

Anuhrad fell back, blood spurting from his mouth.

'BANJAN!'

Hiranya froze at the sound of his name, sweat trickling from his forehead. He saw Anuhrad grinning at him with a bloody mouth.

'It's done now. She's going to kill you. A-HA!' he said as he wiped the blood.

Hiranya cursed under his breath and turned to face Kayadhu. 'Yes, my dear?'

Even now, wisps of soft brown hair framing her lovely face, coral eyes flashing, she looked ethereal in a long, dressing gown, a child cradled next to her chest. Prahlad.

'What are you doing?' she asked, flaring her nostrils.

'I am … uh … training him.'

'He's hitting me!' shouted Anuhrad.

'Why, you!' Hiranya instantly turned to threaten his son who scampered away with a chuckle. He turned back to face his wife. 'No, he's … okay. I was not hurting him. It was part of practice.'

'You know, sometimes I wonder whether you might even kill your own children if you get the chance.'

Hiranya bit his lip. 'I would never do that – I swear.'

'Do you think I believe you?'

'Well, I swear on his life,' he said and placed his big palm over Prahlad's small head.

'No,' she said, grabbing his hand and placing it on her own head. 'Swear on my life.'

Hiranya took a deep breath. 'Okay. I swear on your life – I will never hurt them.'

And then, he woke up, drenched in sweat, anger coursing through him, his heart racing. *I don't feel good.*

And even though he had made the vow a long time ago, he had had a hard time living up to it. He recalled Lord Brahma's third trial and how, unwilling to take the risk that his son would grow up to usher the Asura empire's destructions, he had sacrificed Prahlad. It was an illusion of course, but he couldn't help but wonder if it had been Lord Brahma's way of sharing a premonition about the future.

He bit his lip and rose from the bed. The ship rocked at just that moment, and he felt his stomach lurch – he hated sea travel, which made having a bucket next to him to retch into a necessity.

There was a knock on the door.

'My lord?' Someone from outside peeped in.

'Yes?' Hiranya sighed.

'There is a fleet of ships blocking our path. Perhaps Lord Varuna has heard of our arrival.'

'Is there a lead for the fleet?'

'Yes, a colossal lead – twice as big as our vessel.'

Hiranya nodded. 'Coming.' He walked to the door and went out with his guards. All the other soldiers were waiting to see what he would do. He walked on to the deck to see hundreds of ships blocking their passage, and the lead ship sailing towards them. It was probably carrying a messenger and with him a warning to return.

'Should we wait, sir?' asked the guard on his side. 'Or should we attack?'

'Wait for what?'

'For the message.'

'So they can ask us nicely to leave?'

The guard shut up. The soldiers watched in awe as Hiranya began to chant Lord Brahma's name, causing his armour and his blade to materialize out of nothing. Without a second thought, he leapt out of his ship and on to the water – and *sprinted*.

He had thought he would swim quickly towards the lead vessel, but the armour was allowing him to briskly pace himself as he ran over the water with such speed and power, that he reached the hull in mere moments.

Holding his sword aloft he sliced the ship into two, its occupants floundering amidst the debris in the water.

The other ships began to turn, as Hiranya ran towards them. He had learnt the ways of the Brahmshastra in his spare time, explored its mystical possibilities. He leapt from his position on to the deck of one of the ships. With a quick slash and tug, he managed to create a massive rift through the middle of the ship, all the way down to the hull. Within moments, the ship and its crew were lost to the sea.

Meanwhile, Hiranya continued to leap from ship to ship, whipping though the air.

After taking down more than a dozen ships, Hiranya climbed on to one of the usurped vessels. He strutted about the deck while the Naga soldiers cowered in fear. His body ached, He was invincible.

Around him, the scorched ships, the fire and exploding chaos were not much of a distraction. While he had taken down most of the ships single-handedly, the rest of them were made short work of by his men.

Hiranya turned his attention to the man in front of him. He was a Naga captain. 'Return to your shores,' Hiranya said, his eyes blazing.

The captain meekly nodded.

'And tell your god of the ocean, Varuna, that I'm here and I seek an audience with him.'

The captain nodded.

'Good.'

'Who … who … who should I say wants to meet him?'

'He knows me.' Hiranya smiled. 'After all, we used to be cousins.'

16

CHENCHEN

She had known her life wouldn't be the same once she left the safe haven of Lord Shiva's lands and entered the snowy wilderness where white tigers roared. Ahead of her was the brave Parvati – once a decadent and a hostile woman who hid her glories inside the crevices of her house since her son died and she had distanced herself from humanity inside her home. Now, she was out here. And she was a Matrika.

Chenchen would be a liar if she said she didn't know them. She had read about them – the all-female mercenary group trained in all sorts of combat that had fought for various empires. Each woman was endowed with a particular skill and a weapon that she would use. Created by Lord Indra during the years of the expansion of his rule, the Matrikas parted ways from him when they recognized his clueless vision and blazing tyranny. Chenchen had wanted to join them in their early years when there was more fire in her bones. Years of medical service had taken her prime. Fighting and killing someone was out of the question.

'I didn't know you were a Matrika,' Chenchen said as her horse trudged through the blanket of snow.

'Then I did my job well,' replied Parvati.

They rode up the hill and then zigzagged down. The skies were turbulent, but the blizzard was light. Chenchen clutched her cloak tightly against her chest.

'You wanted to hide that fact?'

'Oh yes. Only Bhairav knew. You see, I married Bhairav because he was going to be a Shiva. It is prophesied that a son of Shiva and a Matrika will be the harbinger of good in this world,' she said. 'Named Skanda, he will represent hope. I was chosen by my brethren to wed Bhairav and once I did, I was supposed to bear Skanda. Unfortunately, things didn't go according to plan.' Her voice was quiet with disappointment. 'First, I bore a stillborn that was disposed as soon as he came to the world. The next was Bhringi, who was supposed to be the famed Skanda, but he also died.'

'Until now,' Chenchen said. 'Do you really think that the man who killed Shiva can represent hope?'

'Now, I don't know.' Parvati coughed. The cold had seeped into her body and her nose was blocked. 'I can only believe. My brethren were disappointed, and we didn't talk until they sent me a letter of condolence with their new location – I knew I had to find them. We still hope to find Skanda, my son.'

'What did the prophecy say, exactly?'

'Skanda will defeat the great dawn along with the help of the seven mothers,' she said. 'The seven mothers being the Matrikas.'

'I see,' Chenchen said.

As they came downhill, the forest grew thicker and white, frosty canopies covered the entire place. The sun was blotted out, and it was biting cold.

'It was supposed to be here,' Parvati said.

As they tried to figure out what to do, there was a flurry of movement in front of them. A bunch of raggedy men wearing loincloths were running for their lives, while being chased by a panther. Chenchen pulled out a small dagger, but Parvati stayed her hand and said: 'Watch.'

What? Chenchen was puzzled.

The panther pounced on one of the men and brought him down. While it chewed on the skins of the men, while another shadow appeared and brought a trident close to the man's cutting it in half. There were a few other shadows, who chased these men until they all sprawled.

And then the animal rested. It growled at them, its whiskers twitching, as it bared its fangs. It was pure black and so beautiful that it didn't seem at all threatening to Chenchen for a moment – until it roared loudly.

'It's okay. Do not let it sense fear or aggression from us,' Parvati said. 'We need to be careful.'

Chenchen nodded, but she could feel her pulse beating faster. She swallowed a lump as the panther casually watched them, flicking its tail. Suddenly, a laughing sound came out of nowhere.

They turned towards the sound and saw six women emerging from the forest, chuckling, even clapping. The panther lay down and began to lick its paws like a tame cat.

'What's going on?' Chenchen asked Parvati, but her question remained unheeded as Parvati got off her horse and started embracing the women.

'A bunch of Nishadhs,' one of the women explained, referring to the forest dwellers, 'tried to steal from us, so we taught them a lesson.'

'Don't worry, it's mine,' said another when she saw Chenchen staring warily at the panther. She was as dark as her onyx hair. She whistled and the panther went back into the forest. 'She likes to scare new visitors. My name is Chamundi.'

Chenchen dismounted and shook hands with Chamundi who, she noticed, had a long trident on her back and a skull hanging by her girdle. Her red lips glimmered against her black skin as she smirked.

A woman wearing yellow satin with a noose hanging on her belt and a lotus-shaped pendant around her neck came forward and shook hands with Chenchen. 'I'm Brahmani, the leader of this group. I'm glad you have come.'

'I hope you are well,' Parvati said.

'Sister, we will be.'

They embraced as if they had not met for centuries.

Parvati asked with a chortle: 'What are you hunting nowadays?'

'Bandits. Got paid by a village to get rid of them. We had just returned from there only to be set upon by the bloody nishadhs.'

'All right.' Parvati nodded, wondering how to broach the reason for her visit.

Brahmani noticed the pensive look on her sister's face. 'What is going on? Why are you here after such a long time?'

Parvati turned to her. 'I think Skanda is alive and out there.'

Everyone went silent for a moment. Brahmani nodded. 'Fine. Let's talk this through.'

They all sat around a bonfire, sharing bowls of soup and vegetables that Chenchen chomped through. Her eyes fell on a Simhi who had the hide of a lion draped over her, and a tough build with claws as her weapon. She was called Pratyangira, but because of the famous Narasimha, she called herself Narasimhi. Jealousy bloomed under Chenchen's skin.

Brahmani, after listening to Parvati, asked, 'Are you sure Andhaka, considered the most evil human being in the world, is the saviour?'

'He's my only child,' Parvati replied. 'And as the prophecy says …'

'I know.' Brahmani nodded.

'I'm sure,' Chamundi intervened, 'the reason he turned out the way he did was because we were not there to be his mothers and take care of him, to guide him. I'm sure he would be a far better person if we all were there.'

Everyone in the group nodded while Chenchen remained silent.

'And why have you brought a manav with you?' Brahmani asked, referring to Chenchen. 'Does she benefit from knowing our location or do we need to get rid of her?'

Chenchen coughed nervously, and all the women laughed. Even Brahmani did as she said, 'We are just pulling your leg, woman!'

Parvati smiled. 'She came to me when I was leaving and when I looked at her, an idea struck me. She can help us. You know why.'

Chenchen didn't understand what Parvati meant, but Brahmani eyed at her with a knowing smirk.

'That's why you brought her?'

'Yes.' Parvati nodded as she turned to Chenchen. 'I apologize, my friend. I have not been honest with you. In fact, I brought you to help us.'

'But how …' Chenchen began, confused.

Brahmani pushed her hair back. 'A sorceress lives in these woods. She has the third eye – she can see what we can't. She can help us locate Skanda.'

'I thought you told me,' Chenchen said to Parvati, 'that the Matrikas might know the location.' She couldn't believe her queen had lied to her.

Parvati looked away to avoid meeting Chenchen's disappointed gaze.

'How can I help? I'm just a doctor.'

'So you are,' Brahmani agreed. 'But you are approximately our age, and you are not a Matrika – not a branded one at least.' All of them showed her their palms on which different sigils had been stamped.

Brahmani continued, 'This sorceress, she demands that people who go to consult her meet these two conditions. Now we can't, but you can. Will you help us?'

Chenchen looked at everyone except Parvati. She still had her food bowl with her, and she could go back. It was a two-day journey. But for some reason, this felt different. This felt important. 'All right,' she said, 'I will. Who is this sorceress?'

Brahmani sighed. 'Her name is Nrriti.'

'Wait ... I've heard of her ...'

Brahmani nodded. 'She's not just a sorceress. She's a divine being, an immortal.' She paused and continued as the fire crackled loudly. 'She's the goddess of death.'

17

NARASIMHA

'This is just amazing,' Garuda groaned, hitting his head against the walls of their cell.

Nara was lying on the bed, looking at the damp ceiling. There were cries and wails from the other prisoners, some of whom were shouting vulgar abuses.

'We didn't really have the most perfect plan, in all honesty,' Nara replied, shrugging.

'So you should have told me that!' Garuda scowled.

'Yeah, but I'm not much of a planner. I never was. I am a good fighter.'

'But you didn't fight!'

'I don't kill innocents and the Nagas were just doing their job,' Nara said.

Garuda grunted. 'Well, boo hoo!'

They had been here a while, and no one had come to talk to them, which only raised Garuda's annoyance, who constantly muttered stuff about his mother.

'I can't sleep nowadays, friend,' he began. 'She would sing lullabies and tell me stories, my Amma.'

Nara smiled. 'You are a kid, you know.'

'I'm my mother's son, and I'm proud of it!' he scowled. 'Not many have the privilege of being so close to their parents.'

Nara nodded. He didn't remember his parents, and sometimes he really regretted it.

'I agree,' Nara said. 'I absolutely agree.'

'You know we are going to be executed, right?'

Nara coughed. He didn't like how his insides felt right now. 'What's the point? We will die from the poison any way.'

'Oh, I had forgotten about that!'

Nara ignored his sarcasm. 'We don't have a lot of time, you know.'

Garuda nodded, showing Nara his palm into which he had been coughing. It was red. 'I'll die quicker since I'm coughing blood now.'

Nara just lay there and wondered how things never went according to plan. 'If only I could have used the somas I had.'

'No, you can't. The somas you use has a lot of adulterants to enhance your power. What you need is the truest form extracted from the Somalata plants. There's a guarded field in the eastern corner of the city where we can find the plants and ingest them.'

Nara nodded. He desperately wanted to get out and get over the effects of the poisoning. He should have just stayed with Chenchen – it would have been for the best. He wondered where she was, what she was doing at that moment.

'I hope they are taking care of her, these shits,' Garuda grunted. 'Amma likes to stay safe, you know? I'm just freaking out now.'

'It's good to see a son who cares about someone other than himself.'

'Of course! Which son doesn't? He who doesn't is not a son,' he said.

Nara heard footsteps echoing down the prison corridor, and saw a silver-haired man wearing a white brutish armour walking towards them. His face was thin and he had pale eyes and his hands were clasped behind his back, as if he were trying to exude a certain sense of dignity. Everyone in the kingdom knew him: Jayant, scion of Indra.

'Hello there,' he said. 'A sight for sore eyes indeed.'

'Ugh!' Garuda grunted. 'Kill me please. Quickly?' he said to Narasimha.

'A Suparn and a Simha together in a cell. Sounds like the beginning of a joke, right?' Jayant chuckled. 'How do you do, boys? You really thought you could just barge in and do whatever the hell you had planned to do?'

Nara expected Garuda to speak, but he didn't.

'We have strengthened our security since the last time you attacked us, Garuda. You should have come better prepared.'

'I did.' Garuda rolled his eyes. 'And I would have gotten away if I wasn't so limited by my friend who doesn't like to fight your men.'

'You were abrasive, and you thought with your heart instead of your brain. You didn't strategize. Nara is an honourable man,' Jayant said. Turning to the Simha, he added, 'I can't kill you. My father won't approve since you are his friend. But I sure can kill him ' He gestured to Garuda.

Nara stood up. 'If you kill him, you kill me.'

'Ah,' Jayant sighed, 'you make it so difficult. FINE! I won't.'

Nara and Garuda grinned at each other.

'Or,' Jayant mused, 'I'll kill both of you and be done with it. I'll just tell my father that your death was an accident. Phew! So before you leave for the death chamber, would you like to say goodbye to your mother, Garuda?'

Garuda came forward. 'Where is she?'

'Right here.' Jayant brought his hand forward from behind his back. He was holding a metal urn.

Nara's heart leapt in confusion. *Wait, what?*

'Don't involve her,' Garuda said. 'She has seen enough.'

'You and your obsession with the dead!' Jayant shook his head as he opened the urn and overturned it. Nara watched aghast as ashes fell to the ground and Jayant stomped all over them.

With a loud cry, Garuda fell to his knees.

Jayant glanced at Nara and realized his confusion. 'Oh, you thought she was alive? Yeah, he talks about her like she is, the lunatic. His mother has been dead for the last ten years.'

18

HIRANYAKASHYAP

He was in the palace, by invitation. He had been granted an audience with the god of this city. So, he didn't mindlessly kill anyone. He wanted a conversation with Lord Varuna, that was all. His army was on his ships, which were sailing around Naglok while his personal guard crowded the streets of the city.

As he walked the halls, he saw the soldiers lined up in their hundreds, spears upright, but ready to strike at any moment. Was he scared? No. He could defeat them all in five blinks of the eye. He entered the throne room, where a dozen soldiers guarded the throne elevated over fifty flights of stairs. The doors behind Hiranya closed.

He had his Brahmshastra. But twilight was approaching. If he wanted to attack, he would have to do it now. But he didn't have the motivation to attack his cousin.

There was a lot of water in each channel on the sides of the room, and it was all greenish as if someone had injected strange colours into it. Varuna sat on the throne, unmoving and unblinking, clad in an outlandish blue garment, and wearing a lot of signet rings and bangles. His hairline was receding, and his eyes, green as seaweed, were the only feature that stood out in his gaunt face.

'It's good to see you, brother,' he called out.

'Are we being so formal that you need your men here?'

'You haven't approached me in the kindest manner.'

'They attacked me first,' Hiranya lied.

'I don't care. You have come here to overthrow me.'

'If that was my intention, Varuna, I would have already done it,' Hiranya chuckled. 'The city is in disarray because of your involvement right now and the people are scared. What's worse, the Nagas are not particularly happy that an Asura was able to breach your defences so easily.

'How did you do it, though? Is it that armour? My men said you walked on water.' Varuna's hands trembled as he asked again, 'How did you do it?'

Hiranya smiled. 'Get your men out of the room, and I'll tell you.'

Reluctantly, Varuna ordered his men to disperse. All the nagas soldiers crossed Hiranya and walked out of the throne hall. 'What is it then?'

'It's called the Brahmshastra, and it makes me invincible. It's something I've earned.' Hiranya paused. 'Thank you for trusting that I wouldn't hurt you.' He bowed a little. 'I wish I could have said the same when you stabbed me in the back in Pataal.'

'You were being an idiot,' Varuna said.

'I was exacting revenge for my brother! I didn't want what happened to him happening to me. And the Asura elders were not allowing me to take a larger army against Indra and Varaha.'

'Yes,' Varuna said. 'Because of me.'

'You said it was a futile attempt. But then you went behind their backs and joined Indra's crusade,' Hiranya spat at him.

'I had to – he's a good man, Hiranya. He's just misunderstood.'

'And I'm not?'

Varuna spoke after a pause. 'You are a flawed man. You only see blood and rage and destruction. You know why I moved to Indra's side? One of the biggest reasons was because you went against what Kayadhu stood for.'

For a moment, Hiranya couldn't believe his ears and began to question himself. Had he changed? 'She was killed by his man, Narasimha, and for that I shall always blame Indra,' Hiranya said, recalling what Agni had revealed to him a few months ago.

'Nara? So you know?'

'Yes. But I hold Narasimha as responsible as Indra,' said Hiranya.

'You know Narasimha is here?'

Hiranya's blood ran cold. 'What …'

'We caught him trying to enter the city, for reasons I neither know nor care about. He was Indra's favourite. Not mine. Take him and be off. It's a one-time offer,' he said. 'My only concern is the city; he means nothing to me. You want your revenge. I'm handing it to you on a silver platter.'

Hiranya thought for a moment, about having his wife's murderer at his mercy, about the many ways in which he could kill him, but it didn't satiate him. It didn't make him feel good or satisfied. It made him realize something. 'I will have him, and I will have this city,' he said, looking at Varuna.

'I knew it! It was never about Kayadhu – she was just a front to conquer all. You are just a raving madman! What has happened to you? Do you think you are a conqueror?'

'I might not have been earlier – but I am now.' Hiranya's lips twisted into a grim smile.

Varuna stared at him for a while. 'I think I shouldn't have sent my men out.'

'I know,' Hiranya said. 'I was lying when I urged you to trust me. My men are attacking the city even as we speak. My ships have turned and are launching balls of fire with their catapults.'

'Why did you want a private audience?' Varuna asked, biting his lip.

Even though he showed fearlessness, Hiranya could see the unsheathing horror in Varuna's eyes. He didn't like being here. He was clearly uncomfortable.

'Because when I squeeze the life out of you, I want to be alone and I want to do it in absolute silence.'

Varuna chuckled. 'Good.' He stood up, no weapon or armour at his side. 'Have you forgotten that I too have a gift?'

Hiranya knew that as a child Varuna had possessed hydrokinesis, the psychic ability to manipulate water. His face twisted in confusion. 'But you weren't able to do it properly because of your paralysis.' Varuna had suffered the problem much later in life.

'Oh, I know but amrit cures paralysis too. Few doses and I was fine.' Varuna grinned as he brought his hand forward and the water on Hiranya's side rose like a tsunami. 'The water contains tetrodotoxin extracted from the puffer fish. I mutated it with a mixture of amrit to create a lethal combination that can break past any armour. And I mean, ANY KIND.'

He began his demonstration by directing a stream of green water across Hiranya's breastplate which created a burning dent.

With dawning horror, Hiranya realized he had underestimated this man. He unsheathed his blade as he prepared for the duel. Winning this one would be tough.

19

CHENCHEN

The woods were filled with ashen colours. She had never seen something like it. Trudging across the plain, Chenchen could feel her heart racing and her throat clamping up. There was something sinister about this place. It didn't feel right. With every step, she contemplated returning to the camp.

But what would I do then? Stop, Chenchen. Think. Perhaps you are here for a reason. Perhaps there's meaning to all of this.

All her life she had been someone tucked in the protection of that fortress and now she was out ... and she felt good. She felt free. But at the same time, she knew why she was doing it. The only person who could calm Andhaka was his mother. And the only way that would be possible was if she, Chenchen, helped the Matrikas.

She knew that she would have felt guilty if she hadn't agreed to join this crusade with Parvati. From the little she had faced with Nara, she knew it was important to be a hero in this bleak world.

A banyan tree stood in front of her, the one she was told to look out for by the Matrikas. Towering over her was the biggest canopy she had ever seen. It had a lot of twisted vines falling out of it, and contorted branches that seemed reptilian. The smell was dense, like ash had been burnt here … and flesh. The ground around her was covered in dead leaves – some of them even bloody.

'I call thee, goddess of death, mother of crows, watcher of night and bringer of the sun, lover of cranes, she who resides for everyone in the end, Nrriti …'

Something in the clearing moved. A gaping hole opened up in the trunk of the tree and from it emerged a leg and then two hands, and then another leg, like a contorted spider crawling out of its hole.

The goddess had dark hair and dark lips, and eyes … well, she had no irises, just pupils pale as the ashen snow that Chenchen stood on.

Chenchen was a woman of science, and she didn't believe in magic except the extraordinary strength of Nara. But seeing this sorceress, this goddess, Chenchen realized she was not from this world. Even the wolves howled when she appeared.

The goddess looked at Chenchen like a hawk, not moving, and the silence brought immediate tension. Chenchen knew that the goddess wouldn't hurt her if she did a few things correctly.

Ask the right question. Don't beat around the bush, even though she would try to distract her from the question.

Don't be distracted. Just don't.

If Chenchen wasn't successful, Brahmani had said that she might not even return to them.

She had to tread carefully. Pulling the words out of her throat, she said: 'Where is Skanda, the hero of prophecy, who will destroy the great dawn?'

Nrriti sneered, her voice like a quiet, snarling whisper. 'It's interesting how you speak of Skanda as a hero even though he isn't one. You know who the hero, the avatar, is. You have always known.'

Chenchen clenched her jaw. 'Where is Skanda, the hero of prophecy, who will destroy the great dawn?'

'Speak of him once again, and I shall kill you.'

Chenchen repeated the question.

Nrriti growled, and then chuckled. 'You have been taught well. Tell me,' she scowled. 'Do you think Skanda is a hero? I see he is not. He's someone who will be a force of good at the appointed time, but he will not be a hero. Noooo.'

Chenchen repeated the same question for the fourth time.

'Do you worship the dead?'

She didn't answer.

'Do you worship the dead?'

Chenchen remained frozen. She didn't know what to do.

'I speak to the dead,' Nrriti giggled. 'You have some bones you have not burnt properly. Tell me, who is … Ranjhana?'

Her heart skipped a beat. *He was my husband.*

'He speaks ill of you,' Nrriti said. 'Says some vile, vile things about you, eeps,' she giggled again. 'TELL ME! Am I wrong?'

Chenchen didn't say anything.

'He says you lie to the living,' Nrriti continued. 'That he was killed by the Mlecchas. Eep, no. No, no, no!'

Chenchen's heart stopped. *No.*

'He says,' Nrriti had a blinding brightly smile on her face, 'it was *you* who killed him.'

20

NARASIMHA

The ceiling above them shook as a spray of dust swirled down on them.

'You didn't tell me your mother is dead!' exclaimed Nara the moment Jayant left, the ashes of Garuda's mother in front of their cell.

He ignored the disturbance happening outside, even though he knew something was wrong. From the sounds and the crackles and the yelps it seemed as if a *revolt* was happening. But he focused here, right now, in front of him where Garuda tightly clutched the bars of his cell, trying to collect the ashes in a torn cloth.

'I thought she was alive,' Nara said to himself. 'Why would you ...'

'Because I like to believe she's still here!' Garuda shouted, his hands covered in ash. 'I like to believe she still pats my head before I bloody fall asleep. I like to believe she still gives me that soup. And I like to believe she's alive. I am not an idiot, Nara.' He clutched the cloth to his chest. 'I know she's dead. I just need to ignore the reality.'

'We all have lost someone, and it is important to accept it.'

'Well, I can't!' Garuda scowled. 'I'm not like you. I'm not – I'm not strong.'

'Do you even have your men waiting at the Suparn hideout? Do you have anyone?' Nara was beginning to think that even the poison was not real inside him, but he did feel his insides churning.

'Of course, they are! I'm not delusional, Nara.'

Just then the ground began to shake. And before they knew, swarms of men entered the prison and began beating up the Naga jailors. Asura soldiers barged in, opened the cell doors and let prisoners out.

'OFF YOU GO! WRECK THE CITY!' they chuckled.

When they reached Nara's cell, they looked at him.

'Oh! Look who we have here,' one of the Asuras chortled, 'a Simha,'

Oh no. Nara had been hoping they wouldn't notice him.

'What is he doing here?' another Asura asked.

'Our king has told us to get rid of any Simhas we come across,' they said as they unsheathed their blades. 'You aren't a Simha. You can leave,' they told Garuda upon entering the cell.

Garuda looked at Nara and, with a nervous swallow, said, 'Sorry, brother. But I have to leave.'

Nara watched in disbelief as Garuda hurried out of the cell, leaving him alone to fight the Asuras. As they charged at him, he deflected their swords with his claws and, bending, tore at their knees. One of the Asuras fell, crying in pain while the other raised his sword and swiped at Nara's neck. Nara punched him in the gut and ripped out his throat, killing him instantly.

By now the fallen Asura had hobbled to his feet and was about to plunge his sword into Nara's back when …

Garuda came and punched him in the head.

Nara turned back to see his friend. 'Why did you come back?'

'I like to give surprises.' He grinned and he knelt next to the guard. 'What is happening?'

The Asura was still reeling from the blow to his head, so Garuda shook him hard.

'What is happening?'

'Madness, chaos. O-o-o-o-our great god is taking over the city, and we are removing any sign of Devas or Nagas or Manavs.'

Nara felt a weird churning in the pit of his stomach. *This is not good.*

'Where is Jayant?' Garuda asked the Asura, punching him again when remained unresponsive. 'Where is the son of Indra?'

'I heard he was going to escape in his vimana from on top of this dun –'

Garuda was already on his feet and sprinting out of the cell before the Asura could finish speaking.

Nara followed him at breakneck speed. 'WHAT ARE YOU DOING?'

'Stopping that shit from escaping!' Garuda yelled back.

The terrace of the prison building was littered with the corpses of Asuras and Manavs who were fighting each other. Amidst the chaos, Jayant prepared his vimana, an elongated machine with wings on the sides, engineered and powered by soma-fossilized stones. He was starting his machine while his men fought the Asuras who didn't have the slightest intention of leaving.

Grabbing a sword from one of the corpses, Garuda ran towards Jayant. Just as the vimana began to lift into the sky, Garuda jumped in, taking Jayant by surprise.

I can't let him go alone. Nara sprinted, his heart beating fast, his body desperately fighting off the fatigue brought on by the poison. He leapt from the ledge of the terrace and landed on the vimana's wing. Jayant and Garuda were locked in fierce combat, and paid him no heed.

I can't let them kill each other.

He began to climb into the vimana, all the while staring at the mayhem on the ground below. Shops were being burnt. The roads were being paved anew with corpses. There were houses being sacked and thwarted. It was absolute chaos. All because of Hiranyakashyap.

In this war, Nara didn't know who was worse – the Devas or the Asuras. But he knew he had to rescue his friend. Once he was inside the vimana, he tried to come in between the two warriors, but Jayant had already plunged his sword deep into Garuda's shoulder Screaming in agony, Garuda gave Jayant a mighty shove as he lurched back to a corner, clutching his injured shoulder. Jayant lost his balance and toppled over the side of the vimana. In his frantic scramble to grasp something, he disengaged the controls. Immediately, the vimana began to spiral downwards. In a split-second reaction, Nara grabbed the lever of the vimana to pull it up in the air, and grabbed Jayant by the other hand, so he wouldn't fall. 'Hold on to me!' he yelled. 'Hold on!'

Jayant held on with both hands, but his grip began to slip. Nara desperately tried to haul him up while keeping the vimana steady with one hand.

'Leave him!' yelled Garuda, who began to push at Nara's fist and tried unclamping it. 'He doesn't deserve to live, this scum.'

'No, I won't,' Nara said. 'He's Indra's son. You have no clue what sort of wrath you will bring ...'

But Garuda didn't listen. He punched a straight jab into Nara's arm, making him break his hold. Jayant fell. Down into the raging fire. In the commotion, a Manav soldier looked up and saw Nara and Garuda.

'A Simha and a Suparn!' he yelled.

Garuda ordered Nara, 'Let's go now. We need to go to the farm where the Somalata plants are grown. Come!'

'You shouldn't have done it,' Nara said, his lips pale. 'You shouldn't have.'

But Garuda didn't care. He steadied his injured shoulder and steered the vimana towards the farm. Away from the corpse of the deva prince.

21
HIRANYAKASHYAP

'You shouldn't have done it!' yelled Varuna as he directed arcs of the poisonous water at Hiranya, who dodged them, rolling back. 'You shouldn't have come here.'

Hiranya had to find a way to defeat Varuna, but he couldn't do it when he was within range of the man's power, where water was his ally and could prove fatal to Hiranya.

He was surprised that the water was able to affect his armour, but then noticed that the small dent that had formed had begun to heal, as if the armour was repairing itself. But Hiranya knew that the armour's ability to self-heal wouldn't be much use if the poison got to his skin. He had to be quick.

He used his blade to deflect Varuna's next volley. Though the poison began to eat away at it, the sword was still taking the assault better than the armour had. He sprinted towards Varuna but instantly, a wall of green water blocked his path. His sword, meanwhile, was being regenerated.

'You are a stain on what Kayadhu stood for,' said Varuna.

'And you let her die!' Hiranya exclaimed.

'It was not me. It was not Indra. It was the Simha.'

'Whoever it was, they will all die,' said Hiranya.

The wall began to move towards him like a tsunami, ready to swallow him. Just as the wave broke and splashed down, Hiranya somersaulted backwards, out of the water's reach. With his light armour, it was easy.

'You won't be able to live through this, Hiranya,' said Varuna.

'I don't care. I need to kill you. I need to—'

But he couldn't say any more as Varuna sent spikes of poisonous water towards him.

Hiranya dodged one, while another pierced his armour and struck his skin. A third flew past his head, grazing his cheek – his whole face seemed to have been set on fire.

Growling under his breath, Hiranya knew he had to find a way ...

Another spike!

Hiranya swung the sword in a circle around him to fend off the flurry of spikes. With each blow that glanced off the sword, the blade was damaged a little more. He had to do something fast. His eyes followed Varuna's movements, the way he used his hands to make the water do his bidding, and an idea came to him. He began to walk forward, braving the streams of water attacking him. The moment Varuna created a wall between himself and Hiranya, the Asura plunged his blade through the water and towards Varuna.

Hiranya felt heat sear through the blade, but it held it's shape long enough to cut off Varuna's arms.

All the water around them died down as blood spurted from Varuna's arms and his screams echoed down the hall.

Hiranya casually walked towards Varuna, who was on the stairs to his throne, whimpering in pain, trying to crawl away from the Asura king. As if escape was even possible. Hiranya scoffed. After a long time, he had actually tasted his mortality. Very closely. He grabbed his fallen sword, which had regenerated, and slowly pushed it through Varuna's heart – just as he had done to Agni, with a smile on his face.

Varuna's face went white, as he saw the light moving away, and his hand tried to grasp Hiranya's arm.

'Where is the Simha?'

'Ugh …'

'Tell me!'

'Ugh … cell …'

Hiranya plunged the blade deeper, watching as Varuna's eyes closed. The god of water, the king of Naglok was dead. He turned at the sound of the doors being opened.

'My lord, we have ransacked the city …' His guards stopped, seeing the blood and the poisonous water all splashed around. 'My lord …'

Hiranya turned, his brows raised. Twilight was upon them. And he wanted to have his armour when he fought his wife's killer.

'Find me the Simha from the prison,' he said. 'His name is Narasimha.'

'But, my lord … we opened the prison doors …'

'FIND HIM!' Hiranya yelled, and walked out of the throne room. He was ready to challenge the man himself.

22

CHENCHEN

Chenchen's body froze at the sound of the name. Ranjhana. She hadn't heard it in a while now.

'Where is Skanda, the hero of prophecy who will defeat the great dawn?' she repeated again as tears began to trickle down her cheeks.

'Tell me,' Nrriti whispered as she crawled over to the fear-struck Chenchen, 'would you like to see him?'

No. Chenchen wanted to say it, but she couldn't. She couldn't let herself be distracted. *This is all a test.*

'I can bring him for you. Right here. Right now. You can see his miserable face.' Nrriti giggled. 'Eeps, he really wants to see you.'

'Where is Skanda, the hero of prophecy who will defeat the great dawn?' she asked again, not straying from the question as she closed her eyes.

'He used to call you a name, eeps. He used to call you Chenchita. Wasn't that your name? Chenchen is just a ... a

pet name you kept for yourself, isn't it? What did he do to
you? Why did you lie about him?'

Chenchen didn't answer, but merely repeated the question.
She didn't hear anything in response and, for a while, she
thought the torture was over. When she opened her eyes, she
found Nrriti standing inches away from her, her foul breath
all over Chenchen's face. She wanted to run away immediately,
but she felt paralysed, as if something had rooted her to the
ground and was not allowing her to go.

Gritting her teeth, Chenchen repeated her question. Nrriti
took a step back. Chenchen could see the goddess was getting
annoyed.

'Chenchita?'

That voice ... Her eyes filled up as she realized who it was.
Coming from behind and standing in front of her was a bald
man with a thick moustache.

Ranjhana.

Her husband.

Chenchen couldn't believe it. Her eyes were playing tricks
on her, but she held her ground.

Not only was her dead husband in front of her, he was
bleeding profusely from a wound on his forehead, where
an axe was embedded, one that was put there by Chenchen
herself. But unlike their last encounter, when he had died
from the blow, he seemed all right now, as if the axe on his
head was a natural embellishment.

'You wanted to hurt me – you always wanted to kill me. I
was Lord Indra's soldier, a proud one,' Ranjhana began. 'I was
a valiant soldier, and you destroyed me and my life. For what?'

She had much to say, but she remained silent. Instead, she asked her question again, looking at the playful Nrriti who stood a few paces away from her.

But Ranjhana intervened, 'Just because I hit you occasionally? Just because this marriage was a sham? You were broken, you were not what I thought you would be – so I did it. I hit you. I hit you many times. But I *loved* you, Chenchita. I did. Hitting you was … a way to express my love for you.'

No, it wasn't. Hitting is wrong. It's not an expression of anything but violence. One cannot justify hitting your partner as a form of love.

'I still remember how I returned on the day we lost the battle. I was drunk and you had made food, and I toppled it and I hit you. But you couldn't take it any more, so you took my weapon and you …' He looked up at the axe on his forehead. 'You killed me,' he paused. 'And then you couldn't have just easily said it was done by you. You would be a murderer and be hanged for killing a national soldier, so you orchestrated the entire crime scene as a home invasion by the Mlecchas.'

Chenchen clearly remembered that day. She had hoped she would never be caught on that, and she never had been. Until this woman in front of her.

'I will never stop hating you. You are a whore, you are a …'

'Where is Skanda?' Chenchen asked, ignoring Ranjhana, realizing this was all Nrriti's attempt to distract her. 'The hero of prophecy who will defeat the great dawn …'

'Impressive,' Nrriti replied with a sly smile, and she snapped her fingers, making Ranjhana's body disappear.

'Very impressive. Many fail this test and show me their anger, but you? You persevered. You act like a Matrika, and yet you don't hold their beliefs or their symbols. Who are you?'

Chenchen didn't speak.

'All right,' Nrriti scowled. 'I'll tell you where Skanda is. But beware, mortal, the information you seek is not what you think it is. Skanda is not who you think it is. He'll come out of the blue, someone no one would expect.'

It could be one of her fake omens, but Chenchen didn't care. She just wanted the information and get out.

'The Skanda you seek,' the goddess began, 'remains with the followers of Vishnu. He is the child of an Asura. Seek him, and he shall bring the great dawn.'

Every step back to the camp was a task for her as her heart was racing. Her body felt weak and her head ached. She was emotionally exhausted.

Chenchen knew she was at the camp when she saw the panther sitting by the entrance, licking its paws indolently. All the Matrikas, who were huddled around the bonfire, stood up at Chenchen's return, looking at her pale face and her dry lips.

'Are you okay?' Parvati was the first to reach her. Taking her hand, she asked, 'Are you hurt?'

Chenchen nodded. 'Yes, I'm okay,' she said meekly. 'She told me everything.'

'What did she show?' Brahmani asked.

She shook her head, still not ready to talk about it.

'Brave of you,' Brahmani added. 'Not many can withstand the power of Nrriti.'

'How is she ...' Chenchen began. 'How is she here? I didn't know goddesses exist. I mean ...'

'There are many strange and mysterious things which have no meaning, but they do exist,' Chamundi said, her dark skin looking oiled against the reflection of the flames. 'Just like somas. We know Indra brought the Somalata plants, but where did he find them? How did he mutate the somas into something that would make someone superhuman? I believe it's all magic. The Avatars, the heroes, the evil ... I believe magic exists on both sides. We just choose to ignore it.'

Chenchen nodded , Parvati by her side. 'What do we do now?' she asked.

Parvati looked up at Brahmani, the leader. The other Matrikas waited for her as well.

'What we are destined to do,' Brahmani said. 'Find Skanda and save this world.'

23

NARASIMHA

They were flying over Somgarh. Or that's what Garuda had called it. It was a farm, a long and wide field of greenery and plants, and no trees. There were a few huts belonging to farmers here and there, but other than that, there wasn't much. The fields, unlike the rest of the tapestry, were blue in colour, like rusted sapphire.

Garuda began to guide the vimana into a descent over the plants. 'There are usually guards here, but they must have gone to the front to fight the invaders.'

'I don't like this,' Nara said from the corner, jumping out the vimana as it landed. There were plants around him, with stems as thick and long as his legs. 'I should be saving the people of Naglok.'

'You can't save everyone,' Garuda said, as he jumped out, a hand over his wound.

'You shouldn't have killed Jayant.'

'He was shit.'

'Well, we will have Indra on our tails now,' said Nara.

'He knew exactly what he had done,' Garuda shook his head. 'You and your idealism. The man threw my mother's ashes to the ground as if they were dust. Is that any way to behave?'

Nara didn't say anything. He walked to one plant and looked at it. It was a pure blue, and it had no petals, just a sapphire bud. He began to squeeze the bud and instantly drank the warm blue liquid that oozed out. As warmth suffused him, he felt ... strong and pure as if the liquid had detoxified him completely.

'When did it happen?' Nara asked, referring to Garuda's mother, when the burning sensation inside him started to fade away. When he got no response, he turned around and saw Garuda collecting a lot of plants rather than ingesting them.

'She died when the Nagas betrayed the Suparns and sided with the Devas. She couldn't believe that her own brethren would go against them,' Garuda said bitterly, holding a handful of flowers in his arms like an infant being cradled by his father.

'Who killed her?'

Garuda shook his head. 'No one. She committed suicide.' Lowering his gaze, he sighed. 'The only reason I revolt and don't give up is because of her. She felt so betrayed that she killed herself, and I can't let her death go unavenged. I have to get her kingdom back – one day.'

'And that's why you take the plants to give them to your people?'

'Many of them have fallen sick after being struck by the poisoned arrows the Nagas use. I can help them,' Garuda said. 'I'm not a bad man, my friend. I'm just a man driven by hatred and rage …'

'Everyone is driven,' Nara said, clenching his jaw. 'What matters is that drive, that passion should make a positive impact in this world. Everyone is fighting for their ideals, their vengeance, but who is fighting for what's right?'

Garuda sternly gazed at him. 'And how does one know what is right?'

Nara sighed. 'One knows, Garuda. One always knows. But we just choose to ignore it.' He paused and said, 'I think we should part ways here. I'll return to the city and help the people.' He knew he couldn't stay with Garuda – he couldn't be around him much longer.

'Stay with me. Those people don't deserve to live.'

'Neither do we. And yet, here we are. We might as well do something worthwhile.'

Nara turned and began walking towards the city. *I don't know how I'm going to get out of here, but I'll find a way.*

The building shuddered and began to collapse. People scattered in all directions in a panic. A couple of Naga women stumbled. They screamed in terror as a massive section of the building broke off and toppled towards them, about to crush them. Suddenly, there was a loud roar and when they looked up, they saw Nara towering over them, holding the section, his mighty arms buckling under the weight.

'RUN!' he shouted.

The women nodded, scurrying away from the scene.

He immediately stepped back and let the debris fall to the ground.

There was chaos and destructions all around. Nara saw some Asura soldiers holding a few Naga men and taking them away from their families. They would probably be making them prisoners of war. He sprinted towards the guards and hurled himself at them, slashing their throats and their chests, tearing off their limbs with his human claws.

'Leave!' Nara yelled at the men, who scurried off immediately.

He was in the middle of the forts and three-storeyed buildings. The streets were red with blood and gore, and piled high with Naga corpses. Ahead, on the bridge, there was heated fighting between the two armies. A small contingent of Naga soldiers had formed a barricade to stop the Asuras – who were twice their size, wore bronze breastplates and silver gauntlets, and carried iron swords – from entering the city. But they were losing.

Nara jostled forward and helped the Nagas push the barricades towards the Asuras. The might of Narasimha was on proud display as he forced back the Asuras with ease.

'Thank you,' the Nagas cried. 'Why are you helping us?'

'Where are they coming from?' Nara asked, ignoring their question.

'The port.'

Nara reached the port to find another massacre in progress. There were huddles of Nagas and Asuras fighting each other, with a handful of manavs holding firm against the demonic forces.

Nara raced forward, his trident which he had gotten back from the jailor's room, hanging loosely at his back. He managed to grab it just as Garuda and he were leaving the prison to find Jayant. Deftly navigating the mayhem he leapt on to the deck of the ship where the Asura guards were on standby. The guards attacked him in a frenzy. With a quick flick of his weapon, Nara stabbed one Asura and tossed him in the corner. He kicked a second attacker and sent him overboard. Faced with wave upon wave of Asuras, Nara crouched and spun his trident in a circle. When he stood a moment later, he was surrounded by the corpses of the Asura guards. A lone archer remained by the captain's wheel, who let loose an arrow. Nara caught the arrow midflight and flung it back at the archer; the arrow lodged in the Asura's eye.

'You have nerve,' a hoarse, husky voice came from behind him.

Nara turned to see a tall, broad man with a thick moustache that hung on either side of his face. He wore a golden armour, a helmet with horns and carried a long sword in his hand. Nara didn't doubt for a moment who this was.

Hiranyakashyap.

'You come aboard my ship and kill my men,' he chuckled. 'They said there was a Simha creating havoc.'

'It's nice to meet you too.'

They were alone on the deck. Nara gripped his trident as he circled around Hiranya, while the battle grew more intense on the shore. The sky was tempestuous too, as if mirroring the mayhem on the ground.

'Are you Narasimha?' Hiranya asked. Hope lingered on his face, he almost wanted Nara to say yes.

And he gave that hope to him. 'Yes.'

There was a slight pause before he asked the daunting question that Nara didn't want to be asked.

'Did you know Kayadhu?'

Nara's blood went cold. 'I …'

'Yes, you do,' he grimaced. 'You killed her, didn't you?'

Nara pursed his lips. He had known karma would catch up with him one day, but he hadn't thought it would be like this. 'I'm sorry. She was trying to … she was trying to attack Indra, and it was my duty to protect him.'

'I believe we all are bound by duty. Just like I am.'

Nara barely had time to think before Hiranya raced towards him with breathtaking speed and precision. He instinctively sidestepped, missing the Asura's blade by a hairsbreadth.

As Hiranya wheeled around to attack once more, Nara punched him with one hand and leapt over him, making Hiranya fall. He charged at him with the trident, piercing his armour.

Hiranya was surprised. 'How is this *possible*? This is Lord Brahma's gift.'

'And mine is Lord Shiva's – we both wield celestial weapons.' Nara grinned.

Hiranya shoved Nara back, flinging him across the deck. The Simha collided with the mast, banging his head on it.

The floorboards rattled as Hiranya stalked over to where Nara lay. Grabbing the Simha, he began to punch him in the face. Nara felt weak --his trident was lost. Kneeling over his enemy, Hiranya grasped either side of his head and began to exert pressure, as if trying to squeeze a melon. Scrabbling for purchase, Nara scratched him with his claws, leaving marks over Hiranya's face, which burnt him. The Asura staggered back, screaming in agony. Seizing the opportunity, Nara made his way to the ledge of the ship, planning to escape. Hiranya was a tougher opponent especially with whatever he was wearing. Fighting him head on would just be…

But before he could leap off the ship, he felt his legs being grasped. The next moment, he had been lifted in mid-air and slammed down on the ground, his spine jarring painfully from the impact. Nara cried out in agony.

Hiranya tried to pick him up again, but Nara kicked him in the torso. Hiranya rolled away. Nara picked himself up and dashed to the ledge again. Hiranya sprinted after him.

`I won't let you go,' Hiranya thundered, tugging at Nara's legs again and pulling him back. `I would have killed you here. And I wanted to,' Hiranya said, wiping the blood on his face. `But you deserve to die on the very ground where you killed my wife.'

And then, with a quick pull and punch, Hiranya smacked Nara right across his face, and the Simha surrendered to complete darkness.

24

PRAHLAD

They stood outside their tent while the wind howled. The moments that passed by seemed like droplets of time, slowly dripping away from the living. Prahlad stood staring at the horizon, arms crossed. The people in the Vishnusena were doing their chores, while the man who would reveal the secret remained hidden in the tent behind him.

'Are you okay?' Dhriti's voice came from the back. Soon she stood next to him and put her head on his shoulder.

'Has he woken up?' Prahlad asked, ignoring the question for it brought up a few answers that he didn't want to give.

'Not yet. He will, though. The doctor says he lost consciousness because he was not able to breathe, his windpipe …'

Prahlad snapped, 'I know, I know – it's my fault.'

'What got into you?'

'I don't know – I have to achieve my goal, no matter how,' Prahlad said.

'But won't you just end up like Narada?'

Prahlad recalled how he had defied Narada for his extremist actions, and he wanted to do something different from him. 'I know, but I believe his spirit was in the right place. I'm not aimlessly murdering people like he was. We are being smart this time. But I also know that we cannot succeed without being ruthless and relentless.'

'I hope you know what you are doing.'

'I'm not okay,' Prahlad said after a pause.

'What?'

'You asked me if I was okay – I'm not.'

'Why?'

'I feel like I belong here, but I also feel there's so much to do around here that we are not able to achieve. We should just go and fight and end the damn war.'

'We don't have the manpower.'

'Then gather armies,' Prahlad said, gazing at her. 'Declare truces and form a collective aimed to end my father's reign.'

Dhriti nodded. 'You are right. We should start forming alliances – we're thinking too small. But ... I always wonder what might happen to us after winning.'

'What do you want, Dhriti? I mean, what do you want in the end?' Prahlad asked.

'I believe I would like to have a fulfilling life ... not just settle down once I achieve this objective. I don't want to fight by myself for long. Rather, I want to command my own force,' she chuckled. 'Like a task force to rid the city of scum.'

'Why?'

'I don't know. Ever since I was young, I've always wanted to lead, to guide people towards doing the right thing,' Dhriti said. 'Instead, I became a cold-blooded assassin, which is funny.'

Prahlad smiled. 'I like that. King Prahlad and Queen Dhriti ridding this world of evil and ruling justly.'

'Ah, are we going to marry? We are just fourteen, Prahlad.'

'Oh well, I really don't mind waiting. I do want to be king once my father is imprisoned or ...' He closed his eyes. He didn't want to kill him, but if there was no choice, he would have to ... He just didn't want to end up in that circumstance.

'And you will be. Just like before. And I *know*,' she said, framing his face with her hands, 'that you will have a great rule.'

Prahlad smiled at her. She was his happy place, and he didn't want to lose her, not in any circumstance.

'He's awake!' Asamanja's voice came from the tent.

They both turned to see the new leader of the Vishnusena urging them to come inside. Following him into the dark tent illuminated by three candles, they stopped close to the bed while the doctor checked on Shand, who was no longer red, but as pale as the moon. His eyes were dark, and though he would wheeze and cough every few seconds, he was breathing fairly evenly.

Andhaka stood in a corner, his hands in front, head bowed, eyes covered with a red cloth. On his right was Kalanemi, who Prahlad had the misfortune to meet once before. He was creepier than Andhaka with his stringy, papery hair and his slimy skin, big eyes and broken jaw. He looked as if he had not been given proper nutrition since birth.

'Please don't hurt me,' Shand said as Prahlad walked over to him, his shadow falling over the minister's face. 'Please leave me alone!'

'If you answer correctly, we will,' said Prahlad, glancing at Andhaka, who didn't come out of the shadows. He wanted Andhaka to do the questioning. 'All right, so ... I would like to know about our treasury.'

'Yes, yes, but your father, he will kill me if I tell you anything.'

'Not if he doesn't find you. We will send you on horseback to the east. Find a place to hide there.'

Shand blinked as if considering the possibility of escape for the first time. 'What do you want to know about the treasury?'

'How much money does the city have?'

'It's foolhardy to steal from it. Madness! It's heavily secured. You also need a key to enter which only your father possesses.'

Prahlad nodded, sharing a worried look with Asamanja and Dhriti.

'Hmm, tell them about the original stamps that you used to mint,' Andhaka spoke, breaking the silence.

'Who's there?' Shand asked. 'Come forward!'

'Tell us!' Prahlad said, holding him by the throat.

'All right, all right!' Shand relented. 'You know how currency has to be constantly minted. There's often an exchange and foreign trading that we do. There are a few copper stamps that were originally used to mint our currency, We haven't changed the designs since the inception of the Asura trade in Illavarti.'

'Where are these stamps?' Prahlad asked.

'In the treasurer's room in the palace. In a safe . Someone could go in and steal them with ease since security is not as tight,' Shand explained.

'And one can enter the royal palace,' Prahlad grinned, recalling his childhood, 'through the sewers that connect to the kitchen.'

'Where I worked!' Dhriti laughed. 'I know how to navigate in there.'

Asa intervened, looking up at Andhaka, 'But what is the point of stealing a bunch of copper stamps?'

Andhaka laughed darkly. 'If we steal the stamps, we can mint our own money, leading to the destruction of the economy in two ways. First, we spread it and create a depreciation of the currency. The value will keep dropping making the economy unstable. Second, hmm, since there will be no original stamps, there won't be a lot of minting for a while and no fresh currency, leading to trade deficits and inflation. The entire economy will fail spectacularly. Farmers will strike, there will be rioting, and the people ... who are our prime motivation, hmm ... will lead a revolt. And if we have the people on our side, the empire will fall.'

'No!' exclaimed Shand in horror. 'You can't do that. That's the worst thing. That'll destroy the entire kingdom.'

Prahlad smiled. He liked the idea. It would take patience, but it would be smart. He leaned forward. 'My dear friend, to create a new empire, one must destroy that empire.'

25

HOLIKA

I can't lose again. Naked, except for the loincloth that covered her private parts, Holika walked to the table and lay face down on it.

'You shouldn't do this, my lady,' Amarka's voice came from her left.

She was in her punishment room. The punishment, though, was not for anyone else but herself. A man stood nearby, wearing a hood and carrying a lash.

'I don't care what you think I should do or not,' said Holika. 'I will do what I think is necessary.'

Amarka grimaced under his breath as the first lash landed harshly over Holika's back.

She felt a searing jolt as if currents of electricity went through her body. 'Just because you lost to your nephew?'

'He got the better of me.'

Another lash.

She could feel the burn on her back. Tears filled her eyes. 'But it's more than that,' Holika replied.

This was so much more than punishing herself for not catching up to Prahlad. It was also not being there for him. And for what she read in the journal that afternoon.

Today was my mother's death anniversary. We don't do anything to mark the occasion. We treat it like it's a normal day. Perhaps that's how you move on. By pretending you are all right until you turn to dust.

But I couldn't. With each year, I grew restless. And when I was seven, I walked to my guruji, Narada, and I told him. 'I'm restless, Guruji.'

He said, 'That's because you haven't done shraadh.'

When I asked what that was, he explained that when someone in the family dies, one should honour the dead and be grateful to them.

I was never grateful to my mother. I asked him why we never follow this custom, and he said it was because my father didn't believe in these kind of rituals.

But I wanted to do it. And so I did. Guruji told me what to do – he called a priest from the local village in disguise and I washed his feet, I gave him food and I took his blessings. I didn't understand how I was showing gratitude to my mother like this, but he just told me to do it. He also told me to feed the crows cooked wheat, which I did. That was nice.

At that moment, as the day was over, I felt good. I felt satisfied as if a burden had been taken away.

But then the memories came. And they left me feeling hollow.

I needed someone. It was already night, and with this hole in my chest, I walked the corridors of the palace to find my father, when I crossed Aunt Holika's room.

Ignoring my natural instinct, I went in, hoping I would not be kicked out.

Another lash.

'Where did you learn of this, my lady?' Amarka asked. 'While you are getting hurt here, the other ministers ask of Shand. They are afraid that the Vishnusena will get them as well.'

'Don't worry, I'll catch them,' said Holika.

Another lash. Sharper and more hurtful than the last.

Her back had become numb by now.

'I had a master back in Pataal. My brothers and I, we had the same master. Lord Svarbhanu, an acharya of the highest Asura order, an elder of their race. He taught us everything,' she explained. 'And he also told us that when we fall short of achieving the truest form of triumph, we must get lashed. So on the training ground, if we lost, we would get whipped. After a while, our backs became stronger and our motivation to succeed never dwindled. You know why?'

Amarka didn't answer. He just waited.

'Because fear dictated us. We were so afraid of getting whipped that we made sure we were always winning,' she said. 'I believe fear is the biggest motivation a human can have. Fear is often reviled, but I think it is important. It drives us. It makes us do things we have never done before.'

She closed her eyes and sobbed. Not because of the lashes, but because she now understood the enormity of what she had lost.

The chance to be a good aunt and a good mother.

I walked into her room, and my aunt looked up. She was reading a book. Her face grew cold at my arrival, but she didn't ask me what I was doing in her room.

'Can't sleep?'

I nodded. I was waiting for her to scream at me, but instead she crooked her finger and signalled me to come to her. I walked over to her and casually sat next to her while she showed me a book of stars, astrology, horoscopes. She explained how we are all shaped by destiny, by karma. How everything is decided before we are born.

It was quite interesting.

'You like it?'

I readily nodded.

'Good.' She smiled. 'Now go back to sleep.'

'Can I sleep here?'

'With me?'

I nodded.

I could see her contemplate the possibility. But then, she shook her head. 'I think you should go back.'

I nodded again, feeling disappointed. I wished she had welcomed me. I was only seven. I missed my mother. And in her absence, I wanted Aunt Holika's warmth. But all she gave me was coldness. Despite that, I still hoped she would read to me again. But she didn't.

She never allowed me to enter her room again. And I kept wondering why.

I still wonder.

The lashes were over. When she stood she could barely feel her back. She walked gingerly towards Amarka as the torturer draped a long cloak over her body, to hide her scars.

'So what are we going to do, my lady? We have no idea what they are up to. We don't know why they have Shand!' exclaimed Amarka.

'You are wrong.'

'What?'

'You are wrong about not knowing what they are going to do.' She smiled. 'Because I know what is going to happen, and I know how to stop it.'

Amarka widened his eyes in delight. 'Perfect! But how? Do you have a spy?'

'More than a spy. I received a letter about the entire plan from a person in their camp.' She smiled as she began to walk out of the room. 'He's reliable, because he's family.'

'Who is it?'

She heard Amarka's footsteps following her. 'You know him,' she chuckled. 'The blind prince, the man who faked his own death to escape Indra – Andhaka.'

26

PRAHLAD

He had never seen so much filth in one place. They had reached the outskirts of the city, close to the sewers, and the amount of waste startled Prahlad. There were dozens of them, stepping into mud, shit and all manner of disgusting things as they crossed a river of darkness towards the huge pipe through which they would enter the underbelly of the city.

'Do you know the way?' Prahlad asked Dhriti, who was leading them.

'I took these routes often a long time ago, when I was spying on the royal palace. I couldn't enter from the main gate, so I would go from here,' she said.

Prahlad nodded. It was funny how she had been a cook in his palace for so many years and he hadn't even realized till much later that she was against the empire. Behind him, Asamanja, Andhaka, and Kalanemi followed with a few soldiers.

But Prahlad knew only one person had to go into the office that belonged to Shand and open the safe. The key was hidden in one of the books on astronomy; Shand loved watching the stars.

They all entered the pipe, one by one. Asamanja's soldiers carried torches that cut through the pitch-black darkness. Fortunately, the pipes were tall enough for them to stand upright.

Prahlad could smell the nauseating stench of dead rats and filth. He never expected that a person from the royal quarters fed from a golden spoon, would be moving in the city's sewers. Still, he followed Dhriti with single-minded determination.

'Thank you for helping us,' he said, turning to Andhaka. 'I mistrusted you, but I was wrong. You are a good man.'

Andhaka smiled feverishly. 'I do what is right, hmm. I must tell you something though.'

'Yes?'

'Your brother. He was not a part of any casualty.'

'Then?' He raised his brows.

'He was killed by—' Andhaka stopped speaking abruptly, his gaze riveted ahead.

Prahlad looked up to see what the problem was, and right in front of them stood Holika with her soldiers, arms crossed and a smile on her face.

No.

The royal soldiers had armed their crossbows, and she directed them to shoot. A swarm of arrows came towards the rebels, most of them finding their mark. Prahlad hit the ground, but he saw Dhriti stagger back wards, clutching her arm. The soldiers on their side were shot down with more arrows. Andhaka and Kalanemi hid behind a long shield that they had brought – as if they expected this to happen.

Prahlad jumped to his feet, pulling out his sword. Looking at the wounded Dhriti and Asa, he shouted, 'Leave! I'll stop them.' He knew that if he managed to buy enough time, his friends would be able to leave. He thrust the sword towards Holika, who instantly deflected the attack.

'You can't defeat me, boy,' she said.

Holika's soldiers came forward to fight Prahlad, and with the little training he had, he deflected their attacks, parrying with and stabbing them, one after another.

One of the soldiers pushed Prahlad against the wall of the pipe, but Prahlad pulled out a small dagger from the other side of his girdle and stabbed him repeatedly.

Dropping the body, Prahlad lunged forward to attack Holika, but she raised a crossbow and aimed it at his face. 'Don't move. I don't want to kill you. Look behind you.'

Prahlad turned around hesitantly. Andhaka and Kalanemi standing beside the corpses of the rebel guards; Dhriti and Asa were nowhere to be seen.

'I believe your friends have left you.'

'Andhaka is here.' He looked at Holika defiantly.

'He's family. *Our* family.'

Prahlad heard a chuckle from behind, and turned to see Andhaka grinning to himself.

'You betrayed us!' Prahlad said incredulously. 'I thought you were against the empire.'

Andhaka shook his head. 'No, brother – *you* betrayed *us*.'

'That's how you always knew,' Prahlad said, turning to Holika. 'I would rather rather kill myself than be killed by you.'

Her eyes softened. 'I don't want to kill you, Prahlad.' And he could see the change in the way she approached him. 'I don't have that power. But you know who does?'

'Who?'

'Your father,' she said, 'and he's going to be here soon.'

27
NARASIMHA

He had lost count of the days that had passed since he was captured.

When he had woken up from his brief period of unconsciousness, he was met by the closed doors of the cell underneath the ship. He looked out of the circular window to see endless water, just waves and sky as far as the eye could see. He felt weak so he slept again. When he woke up, it was only to be dragged towards the city gates and imprisoned in another cell.

He hadn't met Hiranya again, nor did he want to. He had never experienced the kind of rage the Asura king felt towards him. Although, it was understandable. Hiranya had already been traumatized because of Nara, and if he found out that Nara was behind Anuhrad's death too … The havoc it would cause was unimaginable.

Nara looked around his cell dourly. The only light was from a crack in the ceiling. The dungeon had more guards than prisoners, probably because they knew how tough Nara was. Even without his trident, which he had lost on the ship, and his claws, which had broken during the fight but would grow back soon, he was a formidable opponent.

'You are special,' whispered a prisoner from the next cell.

'Why do you say that?' Nara asked, leaning back against the wall, hoping to see the man's face, but failing.

'They have these security measures for you. Are you strong?'

'I don't know what I am.' He shook his head. 'I just know I'm a man of regrets.'

'As am I.'

'What happened to you?'

'Lot of things. Gods! Lots of things,' he chuckled. 'Do you have a lady waiting for you?'

'Not so much as waiting as living without me and staying happy. I want that for her.'

'I'm sure you do,' the man said gently.

'She didn't want me to come here.'

'Then why did you?'

Nara paused. He didn't want to tell a stranger about his plan. 'I was brought here. I am not a good man, and the empire knows that.' He had no mane. Worse, it had been taken away from him. Right then, he felt naked and disgusting.

'What dies is reborn,' said the man, abruptly.

Nara turned to him. 'Why would you say that?'

'Here we are, in the worst possible state of our lives, living in this gutter, this stench, and finding solace in our mutual obscurity,' the stranger said. 'We are dead right now. But we shall be reborn.'

'As what?'

'Heroes, the followers of Lord Vishnu,' he said confidently, with finality.

'Lord Vishnu? Are you a bhakt?' Nara asked curiously.

'Yes, I am.'

'Tell me, did Lord Vishnu plan this for you?' Nara clenched his teeth. 'Do you think he wanted this to happen to us?'

'He has a plan for everyone.'

'Gah! I feel he enjoys our misery,' said Nara bitterly. 'He's a sadist.'

'Unwise words from a Simha.'

His blood ran cold. 'How did you know?'

'Your beard. It's growing in a very distinct colour – unlike a Manav's.'

Nara touched his stubble and shrugged in agreement. It was quite identifiable.

'Didn't Lord Vishnu create Simhas to be his followers and carry out dharma in their motherland?'

'Well, time changes people,' Nara said. 'I follow what's right.'

'To you, I believe, but not to Lord Vishnu.'

Nara could hear the accusation in the stranger's voice. 'Is that so?'

'We are born because a good person can never die. He can be trampled upon, broken, tortured, but never fully incapacitated because he always has the blessings of Lord Vishnu,' said the stranger. 'A good man is immortal.'

'But good men often die and evil lives on. Look at how the Asuras are winning.'

'Death is not the end but merely a pause. Often, one believes we cease to exist after death, but we eventually become another individual. Before Lord Vishnu died, he said he would return whenever the world was at its bleakest, when evil started winning. He would return and fight for dharma, for order against chaos.'

'The Avatars.' Nara's hand involuntarily traced his chest where he still didn't have the Shrivatsa symbol, the one that would say he was an avatar.

But Indra believed so deeply in Nara, that he would definitely be one, even though Lord Rudra had told him of a secret – of never letting the avatar walk on this land.

And yet, Nara had. *Perhaps I'm not the avatar. Perhaps Indra was wrong,* he thought. 'How does one know he is an avatar? I mean …' he hesitated.

The stranger sighed and thought for a while before replying, 'I think one becomes an avatar by their deeds. And the deeds cannot be once in a lifetime; they must be consistent. Any person can claim to be good by doing one good deed but it takes much more to be a great person by consistently doing the right thing. And it's tough, because nothing is easier than doing the wrong thing.'

'How do you know so much about this? Who are you?' Nara asked.

But before he could get a response, two guards walked past his door to the stranger's cell.

'Lord Hiranyakashyap seeks an audience,' one of them said.

The stranger walked out of the shadows and allowed himself to be bound by the guards. Before he was taken away, he looked at Nara. Shocked, the Simha realized that his was not the face of a man, but a boy, around fourteen, slender yet tough, as if he had gone through a lot.

'You really don't have to bind me,' the boy said as they walked away, 'I will not run away. I'm as excited to meet my father, as he would be.'

Father?

Nara felt a chill down his spine. The person he had wanted to meet all throughout his journey to Kashyapuri had been right there in the next cell – *Prahlad*.

28

HIRANYAKASHYAP

'You found him?' Hiranya asked as soon as he laid eyes on Holika.

'Yes, we did, brother,' she replied, following him into his office.

'How is he?' Hiranya turned to her with concern.

'He's all right. He's on his way.'

'But why was he in prison?'

'Because,' she paused, as if she had a hard time speaking, 'because he's a criminal.'

Hiranya leaned back. He had been travelling for days and his body felt exhausted. He had stayed awake through most of his return journey as he stationed his men all over at Naglok, finally securing the stronghold. His next, and final, destination was where Indra rested – Devlok. And he would capture it – once he dealt with this problem. 'He's my son,' he said as exhaustion gave way to anger. 'He needs to be free.'

'You can free him,' said Holika simply.

'How?' asked Hiranya.

Holika paused, 'I would say straighten him out but don't kill him.'

Spoken like a true aunt. He smiled. 'I've thought about it and I'll spare him if he admits his mistake.'

She nodded and smiled back. 'It's good to see you again, brother. You've outdone yourself by conquering Naglok.' She stepped forward, embracing Hiranya tightly.

'I killed Varuna,' he whispered in her ear.

'The traitor had it coming.'

'And I found Kayadhu's killer.'

'Indra?' She raised her eyebrows.

He shook his head. 'The man who executed her. He's a Simha. Quite strong for his age.'

'And what do you plan to do with him?'

'I don't know. I'm not going to let him die.' He shook his head slowly. He had just captured a wild animal and was all set to play with it.

'I had originally planned to murder everyone from his race, since they spell the end of my life.'

Hiranya had told her about the journey, the rules to his invincible armour and the final enemy he would face.

'Could this prisoner be that enemy?'

'I will not let him be one,' Hiranya growled and Holika flinched. 'I will kill Narasimha's people, all his men, in front of him. I will bring all the Simhas and impale them in front of him before I gut him like a pig for murdering my wife.' He grit his teeth, burning passion coiling inside of him.

'I would suggest you do it now or risk losing him,' said Holika.

'Revenge borne out of patience is often more satisfying than a quick execution. Recklessness is a failed man's attempt,' he scoffed. Leaning back against the wall, he added, 'Did you find anything in the journal?'

Hiranya saw a hint of nervousness on her face as she gulped.

'I have been a bad person, right, brother?'

'Why would you say that?' he asked. 'Did you ... read something in the journal?'

She shook her head. 'The journal is just his personal history to the point when he was about to be executed. Nothing else.'

He nodded. 'How did you apprehend him?'

'With my help,' came a voice from the shadows in his office.

Hiranya, startled, pulled out his ordinary iron weapon since he didn't have his Brahmshastra on. Standing in front of him was Andhaka, just as he had last seen him.

'How ... wait ... what? You are alive?'

Andhaka smiled. 'Yes, I am, my lord.'

Hiranya started to embrace him but stopped, knowing Andhaka hated physical contact.

'Why were you hiding like this?' Turning to Holika, he asked, 'Did you know?'

She shook her head and said disinterestedly, 'He never ceases to startle me.'

'Just wanted to have a bit of fun with my favourite uncle,' Andhaka chuckled.

'Of course,' Hiranya beamed, elated that his family members were coming out of hiding.

Holika told him what happened and how Andhaka had saved them.

'I apologize for losing Sonitpur.' Andhaka bowed. 'And for not being able to protect Anuhrad.'

'You have protected one of my sons by bringing him back and for that I am obliged. As for Sonitpur, that stronghold was only useful while the Pashupatastra existed. Once it was destroyed, we had no reason to hold ourselves in the north,' said Hiranya.

'Bringing him back? Your son?' he asked, confused.

'Prahlad.'

'Ah, but I fear I might come off as insolent when I say he's no longer your son, my lord,' he exclaimed.

Hiranya arched his brows. 'And why would you say that?'

'He has turned against you. He's angry at the empire and its ideals. He even killed Shand, claiming that the world should be cleansed of Asuras,' Andhaka said.

For a moment Hiranya stood stock-still before he sat heavily on the chair, looking blankly at the wall. 'Are you sure he killed Shand?'

'Out of spite, just to show he was against the Asuras.'

'But he's my son!' Hiranya exploded, his voice echoing off the walls and he pounded his fist on the table. He huffed and held his head. 'What will I do? I can't punish him with death penalty.'

'I have an idea,' Andhaka coughed. 'Might I tell you a story?'

Hiranya didn't answer, but Andhaka began.

'There was a king called Yayati. He was a very flamboyant king, who had two wives and a son each from them. He favoured one wife excessively and did not care for the other. The other wife, lonely and ignored, complained to her father, who put a curse on Yayati, saying that he would be old and never be able to relish his youth.'

He paced across the office hall slowly as he continued, 'The curse weakened Yayati and he wasn't able to rule. But there was a way, the only way, to escape the curse. He could pass it to one of his sons. But the neglected son, Yadu, rejected him out of spite. The king then went to Puru, his righteous son, who accepted the curse and became old. Yayati lived a happy life, filled with glory and conquests, and expanded his kingdom. For all this, he sacrificed the only son he loved by passing a horrible curse to him.'

Hiranya clenched his jaw. 'What are you trying to say, Andhaka?'

'That, my lord, you are at a crossroad right now. You must either kill Prahlad and become the most powerful warrior the world has seen and continue your conquests forever, or lose yourself with the love of a father, letting Prahlad carry on with his whims while you slowly corrode like the cursed Yayati.'

Hiranya glanced at Holika who was quiet but clearly not in favour of Andhaka's idea. The silence was broken by a knock on the door. Holika opened it to a guard, who said, 'My lady, Prahlad is here. He's waiting in the dining hall, as you had requested.'

'Dining hall?' Hiranya raised his brows.

'The boy was famished. I thought I would offer him some food before you talk to him,' Holika said.

'If he has come,' Hiranya spoke loudly, 'then I will decide what to do about him right now.'

Holika closed her eyes, praying his decision wouldn't end badly.

29

CHENCHEN

Things had taken an unexpected turn. Although the Matrikas and Chenchen knew that Skanda was with the followers of Vishnu, the Vishnusena – a populist rebel army hell-bent on finishing the asura empire through unorthodox ways – they didn't know their precise location. It was rumoured that the rebels were camped close to the capital city of the asuras, Kashyapuri.

To find out, Chamunda had asked them to find the trickster, Namuchi. Chenchen had heard of him – he was a ballad singer, a day-to-day traveller who had also worked in different wars with various identities, sometimes as a soldier but mostly as a spy. Namuchi was an all-knowing trickster who would keep a track of people and take money for information he collected. Information about *everything*.

Chamunda had suggested looking for Namuchi along the way to the south, as they crossed the outskirts of Yakshlok.

He had last been seen in one of the nearby villages. She had claimed that he might know where Vishnusena was.

Brahmani was against it while Parvati was all for it, for it would mean being closer to her son. Chenchen had never seen such hunger in a person. Perhaps, she would feel the same way when she had children. She had always imagined having two kids – one boy and a girl. And she would adopt a third one. The thought of having children always made her sentimental since in a war-torn country, it only meant putting them in harm's way.

Chenchen had been in her camp for a day when Chamunda returned, dismounting from her panther.

'I asked around for a slimy sniffer by the name of Namuchi who had one good eye,' said Chamunda. 'Many didn't know who I was speaking about but one brahmin priest did remember serving a one-eyed thief. It's probably him.'

'So he was here?' asked Brahmani.

'Of course he was here. I remember hearing about it from one of the villagers we were helping,' said Chamunda.

Chenchen hated the place. She had never expected to be so unhappy coming to the sand-ridden place from the cold, windy lands. She knew she would be bothered by the heat, the humidity, the endless amounts of sand, but not this. Never this leaden feeling.

'But the bad news is, he has been taken by one of the Kimpurushas.' Chamunda sighed.

'Kimpurushas?' Chenchen turned to Brahmani, instead of asking Parvati, since they were still not talking.

'It's a tribal race,' Brahmani replied. 'They worship horses. They have the best, fastest stallions you could ever ride. Most of the Devas' cavalry are of Kimpurusha ancestry. They have a special connection with the horses, and some say they speak their language. But Kimpurushas were mostly stationed in Devlok, weren't they?'

'Yes,' Chamunda replied, 'but these priests said this lot has turned into bandits. Their enemies about their whereabouts and they were ambushed. The ones who survived caught Namuchi and took him to the White Mountains.' She pointed at the misty hills which stuck out like a sore thumb, too white for the desert wasteland.

'We need to rescue him?' one of the other Matrikas asked.

'The Kimpurushas would have killed him by now.'

'They are torturers.' Brahmani shook her head. 'They'll take their time to hurt the person who ratted on them. Anyway, we should get going. It's almost night and we can apprehend them or buy him off. We'll figure it out.'

Everyone started getting ready with their weapons. Chenchen ignored Parvati's steady stare. As she mulled over her involvement in the entire mission, Brahmani came to her and handed her an iron sword.

'You'll need it.' She smiled.

'But ... but I am a doctor. You don't think I can join this crusade?'

'Well, you are here and we need all hands since we are dealing with bandits. I think you are a fighter at heart.'

Chenchen looked at the sword. She had never hurt anyone with a blade except ...

Her husband.

It was wrong, to kill someone and get away with it. And not be caught.

Can I use a blade for the right reasons now?
She smiled hesitantly. 'Okay.'

They were standing on the a large canyon in the mountains which had a downward slope. They could see the Kimpurushas boozing and dancing to the tunes some of their band played. Dozens of horses stood nearby, their coats shinier and muscles stronger than any breed Chenchen had seen before.

There were two ways to reach their camp. One was the main approach road where guards were stationed, aware and armed with long, twisted blades. Torches illuminated the entire area, discouraging any sudden attacks.

The other way was to swim across the lake to the rear of the camp where Namuchi was being kept. His cage was just a shadow from this far distance.

'All right, I have a plan,' Brahmani said. The Matrikas had grouped together in a circle, including Chenchen, who was feeling different wearing the girdle heavy with the blade. 'The Matrikas will take the main road and distract the Kimpurushas while the two of you' – she pointed at Parvati and Chenchen – 'will swim from the lake and open the cage. Once you are done, we will escape from there as well. All good?'

'What if something goes wrong?' Parvati asked.

'We fight and kill every last one of them.' Brahmani shrugged. 'Let's hope we don't have to be violent tonight.'

They nodded in unison and went in opposite directions. Chenchen silently followed Parvati towards the lake.

'You won't talk to me, now?' asked Parvati.

'I will, my lady, but only if ask me a question.'

'I know you are angry, and I should have told you.'

Chenchen was quiet for a moment. Then, softly, she said, 'I would have come anyways.'

'But what if you refused? I couldn't take that chance. Anyone would be scared to visit Nrriti, but you were quite brave.'

Chenchen gave a hard smile but did not speak again. They reached the lake and began to swim. She had swum long ago and she tried to move her arms and legs in rhythm, pushing away thoughts of how deep the water was. She glanced at the camp where the Matrikas were pretending to be damsels in distress who had lost their way and were in need of protection. The Kimpurushas, who were mostly male, were clearly excited to see female company in their camp.

Chenchen swam harder than Parvati, as if it was a race. Her wet clothes weighed her down and made it difficult to move quickly. Still, she reached the shore moments before Parvati. They caught their breath and began to move towards the cage in a crouch, past the sleeping horses who were tied up to the ground. Cautious of waking the horses, they tiptoed softly to the cage and began examining the locks.

Inside was the so-called extraordinary Namuchi with a bald head and one functioning eye, dazed and distressed. When he saw Chenchen and Parvati, he grinned. Chenchen realized he didn't even have teeth.

'Thank you, thank you,' he breathed without caring to ask who they were. He just wanted to be free.

'Let me tear it open while you keep an eye on the camp,' whispered Parvati.

Chenchen nodded, staring at the scene a few yards away where Brahmani was charmed the dirty Kimpurushas who were offering them wine and food.

BANG!

Chenchen felt as if her heart had been wrenched out of her chest. She turned around and saw that Parvati had used her sword to break open the cage. The sound woke up the horses. They neighed loudly and the Kimpurushas all stared back at their stallions, to find the two women opening their cage.

'It's a trap!' yelled a bandit.

'Go, go!' Chenchen shouted at Parvati, who grabbed hold of Namuchi and rushed towards the lake.

As Chenchen started to follow them, she realized the Matrikas were fighting the Kimpurushas, some of whom were coming towards the three of them. Instead of staying to fend them off, she rushed to the horses and cut them loose. Riled by the noise and commotion, the animals ran here and there, trampling the Kimpurushas who worshipped them. Chenchen turned and saw that Parvati and Namuchi had made it to the shore unhindered. As she set off to join them, she was pulled back all of a sudden. She stumbled and fell.

One of the bandits had escaped the stampede. Just as he raised his blade to stab her, his head was cut off from behind and it flew like a ball, falling on the ground unceremoniously. Chenchen looked up at her saviour: It was Parvati.

'Thank you,' she smiled, taking Parvati's outstretched hand and hauling herself upright..

And after a long time, she felt they had shared a genuine sense of friendship. But by then, Namuchi had begun to swim away, trying to escape.

'Ungrateful bastard,' exclaimed Parvati and then looked at the Kimpurushas coming towards them. 'You get Namuchi and I'll handle the bandits.'

Chenchen nodded and dived into the lake, propelling herself towards Namuchi. She let go of her sword in the water to swim faster and, when she was close enough, punched Namuchi in the head.

'Don't you dare leave!' She got a hold of him and started hitting him on the head. 'Don't you dare.'

'Okay, sorry, sorry,' he heaved.

Holding him by his hair, Chenchen towed him to the opposite shore where she shoved him on the ground. The small, slimy man was no taller than five feet, but now, curled up and shivering, he seemed dwarfish.

'What do you want from me, woman?' he asked. 'I don't know anything. I don't know you or your friends who helped me.'

'I want to know where the Vishnusena is.'

'That's expensive information.'

Chenchen slapped his face hard and then punched him on the nose. She realized that for the first time, she was hurting someone instead of healing them.

'Now? Have you received your payment, you ungrateful vermin?'

'Fine, fine, just because you helped me,' Namuchi grunted under his breath. 'They just shifted their base, since, I don't know. I know a few traders who dealt with them, giving them food and other essentials. They gave me the coordinates of the place. I can write them down for you.'

Chenchen smirked. 'Thank you.'

'There was another one, a blind guy. He threw me to the wolves once I gave him the location. But the Vishnusena had moved on from there,' Namuchi said. 'I hope you don't do the same.'

'Do you see any wolves or hear any howls?' Chenchen demanded. 'Was it Andhaka?'

'I don't know. I don't ask names.'

'Fine,' she sighed, and realized with a smile that under the moonlight, her adventurous spirit, the one that had been caged for so long, was finally liberated.

30
PRAHLAD

He ate as if he had never eaten before. A piece of bread, mashed veggies and roasted potatoes were already stuffed in his mouth, but apparently that wasn't enough. He grabbed an apple and bit a large chunk out of it. He would always end his meal with a bite from an apple.

He was still surrounded by the guards. If he made a run for it, he could break free. But he didn't. He couldn't. In the wild, he had been forced to eat stale and mouldy food but here everything was so delectable and fine. He missed his life as a royal prince.

He reined in his thoughts. He couldn't be drawn to worldly pleasures when he had reached the peak of being a good person instead of a stereotypical Asura.

His hands were still bound and he was stuffing more food in his mouth when he heard the loud footsteps. He would know it anywhere, the sound of his father's footsteps. Every step had a gravity, pushed against the surface.

Prahlad looked up at his father who stood with his hands clasped behind his back. He had thought he would be embarrassed or a shamed in when they finally met, but he felt proud. Because, for once, he was not on the wrong side. Clad in a black kurta and golden dhoti, hair flowing freely and moustache twirled into points, his father towered over him. With a pang, Prahlad realized how much he had missed him. He was desperate to embrace his father, but he was an Asura emperor and Prahlad was a rebel who wanted to topple him. They were meeting as enemies.

Hiranya looked at Prahlad's bound hands and instantly directed one of the soldiers to free them.

As the circulation returned to his numb fingers, Prahlad looked at the deep, red marks over his wrists. Silence permeated the moment as both father and son wondered what to say to each other.

'How was the food?' Hiranya asked awkwardly.

'It was … nostalgic.'

'You have changed. You look …' Hiranya knit his brows together.

'Dirtier?'

'Older.'

'It's been months.' Prahlad shook his head. 'How was your crusade to Yakshlok?'

He paused, pursing his lips. 'It wasn't worth losing you to the terrorists.'

'They are not terrorists, father,' Prahlad said quietly.

'Any one who threatens the national interest with their extremist religious views is a terrorist,' Hiranya thundered. 'And now, you are one of them.'

Prahlad nodded absently. 'I know. Are you expecting an apology?'

Hiranya clenched his teeth. 'You don't mean to give one, I suppose.'

'No, I don't regret it,' said Prahlad, taking another bite of the apple.

'Is being insolent a prerequisite to enter your terrorist organization?'

'They are not terrorists, father,' Prahlad insisted, abandoning his carefree tone. 'They are good people and they have a good cause.'

'What is that cause? To bring down my empire? Do you think it will be that easy?'

'Perhaps not, but it will be worth it.'

'Why are you so against me? What have I done to deserve such hate, son?'

'Nothing. In fact, you are a great father. But you are an unstable ruler. The people want harmony, not war. The casualties they suffer because of your iron fist rule are tremendous.'

'Peace is overrated, believe me. No one can be at peace all the time.'

'I will make sure there is peace.'

'You'll rule without the Asura name once you end me?'

'Yes, I will make sure that we live in the greatest period of our lives.'

'You are delusional, but ah, how is that your fault? You are impressionable, you are weak and you are young.' Hiranya shook his head. 'It will take me a month to change your mind.'

'I might be young but I'm not stupid, father,' Prahlad retorted. 'Once this dead and broken city has been snatched from the grasp of the Asuras, the very stench of it will be removed. I will create a peaceful land of righteousness, of dharma, of Lord Vishnu. And if you get in our way, I will stop you because I am no longer naïve, father. I see the light. I see the goodness that will prevail over you.'

'How dare you speak like that to your king?'

'Because I must.'

Hiranya banged his fist against the table, staring into Prahlad's eyes. 'I'm beginning to think Holika was right in wanting to execute you.'

'You can't kill me,' Prahlad said confidently, 'Lord Vishnu is with me.'

Hiranya scoffed, 'Really? Where is he, eh?'

'He's here. He's with me. He's with you. He chooses even the worst of people and makes them good. While I allow it, you don't. You succumbed to the pain of mother's death, using her to justify your sinister plots, your destruction. Mother wouldn't have wanted this,' he said, eyes raging with passion.

Hiranya didn't respond. Instead, he poured out wine in a goblet and took a sip. Prahlad was afraid. He could feel his bones turning cold, but he was also confident that he would win. He wouldn't die. Lord Vishnu was with him.

'Fine,' Hiranya nodded, 'So let it be. I wanted to give you a second chance, but we are no longer family. Unfortunately, I have lost my son in the war. All my sons. In front of me stands an infidel and he shall be dealt with as an infidel ought to be. Prahlad, for the crimes of killing officials, asassinating the minister —'

Which minister, thought Prahlad, *I let Shand escape on horseback as promised.*

'—inciting extremism and being a traitor to your kingdom, I hereby sentence you to the death' Hiranya declared.

As the guards crowded around Prahlad and proceeded to tie him up, Prahlad saw the sadness brewing in Hiranya's eyes.

'The sentence will be executed by crushing the rebel under an elephant's feet *today*,' Hiranya added.

Prahlad felt the icy touch of death grasping at his throat, as Hiranya smiled coldly, erasing any trace of sadness he had possessed seconds ago.

'Let's see if Lord Vishnu is able to prevent this or not.'

31

NARASIMHA

I have to get out of here.

He had been *this* close to being where he was destined to be at this moment – to protect Prahlad. But now, Prahlad had gone to his father.

What is happening right now?

He grasped the bars on his cell and tried to pull them apart but they were solid iron. Nara had to think of something. He knew he was not a good man. He had set out to do the right thing but had been derailed into this wild goose chase to save his life from the poison he accidentally ingested. He didn't understand why these things were happening to him.

But if the path was simple, anyone could follow it. The tougher tasks were for the people with perseverance, who didn't give up. And for those with luck on their side. His ears prickled as he heard footsteps. The footsteps were light, like a dancer, but also of someone who knew that their footsteps mattered a lot.

'Who is it?' Nara called out.

'Who else?'

Nara's blood went coldas the bald-headed, red bandanna–wearing Andhaka revealed himself. 'I…I …'

'Yes, you killed me and yet, here I am,' he chuckled.

'How?'

'Long story.' Andhaka smiled. 'How are you doing, Nara?'

'You know my name.'

'Of course, I do. When I learnt a Simha was here, I was intrigued. I wanted to see for myself whether it was you or someone else. Simhas are an interesting race, especially you, who came so close to actually killing me. But you failed,' he paused, a thin rasp emerging in his tone. 'It's surprising how destiny brings us face to face with people that matter. I'm intrigued.'

'What do you want? I'm not a puppet to soothe your curiosity,' Nara spat.

'Oh please, you are more than that.' Andhaka grinned, giggling to himself. His thin, feminine voice gave Nara goosebumps. A shiver ran down his neck. 'You are a hero.'

Nara shook his head. 'No, I'm not. I have killed so many innocents. But I seek to redeem myself.'

'In the name of what you felt was right,' Andhaka scoffed. 'Being right is subjective. Remember that or you'll always be on a fool's errand to be the good person when you might already be one.'

The words hit Nara like a rock.

'Tell me, why are you here?' asked Andhaka.

'You'd have to walk over my dead body to learn that.'

'I just might!' Andhaka giggled. 'Fine, you might not tell me, but I can help you, if you do.' Andhaka pulled out a key. 'I got it from the warden. I thought I would take some … volunteers for my cause but I can free you, as well, if you want.'

'Why would you do that?'

'Because you are more interesting in the outside world. That my uncle wants to break your spine is of no particular interest to me. I want him to suffer, whether for wrongfully killing his son or by losing his wife's killer.'

'Son? Where is he? Is he being executed?'

'Ah,' Andhaka breathed. 'So that's it? It's him you are interested in. You want to gut him like you did Anuhrad?'

'No,' Nara protested, 'that was an accident.'

'Sure, sure.' Andhaka nodded. 'He's not a bad boy, Prahlad. He has the right noble intentions in his heart. Now he stands against his father.'

'Really?'

'Yes. He knows his father is wrong and he works with the Vishnusena.' Andhaka told him about the so-called rebels and by the end of it, Nara was keen to meet them. 'Do you want to kill him?'

Nara realized that if he told the truth, Andhaka wouldn't let him go as this would rob him of the opportunity to torture Hiranyakashyap.

'Yes. I want to. And I want to do it in front of Hiranya, just like I killed his wife and his other son. Imagine his suffering.' Nara grinned maliciously.

Andhaka nodded. 'You intrigue me a lot. If you hadn't tried to kill me, I would actually hire you as a guard.'

'Let me kill Prahlad, Andhaka.'

'And what if you kill me when you get out of here?'

Nara paused. He wanted to. 'You can only trust.'

'Trust someone who tried killing me once?' He chuckled as he opened the doors of the cell. 'Run free.'

Nara froze, unable to comprehend what had happened. He stepped out warily, unsure if this was all real or not.

'Go to the top. There's a ladder on the eastern part of the tower,' Andhaka said. 'Climb down from there. You'll meet two guards but they are better than the guards who scout these areas. You are lucky since this is a lunch break. He paused, then added, 'Also, Prahlad is leaving for his public execution at the main bazaar. Go and kill him. I am not sure whether my uncle will be there or not. But he will hear of your deed shortly after you do it.'

Nara nodded, gazing at the blind man.

'I can hear your heartbeat. You want to kill me, don't you?' Andhaka smiled. 'Well, here's the fun part. You can kill me and regret that you killed an innocent volunteer working for the actual Andhaka or you can kill Andhaka, the real one, who I ...' he paused, 'might be. Would you take that chance?'

Nara's hand was shaking. He couldn't do that.

'Why do you hate your uncle so much?' Nara asked.

Andhaka stopped grinning. 'To know that, one must go to my ancestral home, the place I used to stay,' he said. 'It's south of Kashyapuri, and if you want to, really, you might seek it. But the answer to my cause is an absolute travesty for it is quite simple. But aren't simple things often complicated?'

Nara shook his head and began to race to the top, leaving the cell behind him.

I'm coming for you, Prahlad.

32

PRAHLAD

He walked the same path. The same people. Disdainful and hateful against him, throwing rotten apples and other produce that he tried to dodge.

Holika walked next to him, just like before. But oddly enough, there was no sign of hostility or smugness. She was silent as she escorted him to the spot of his execution. It was a circular arena where a large elephant was waiting for him. The instrument of his death. People had gathered in the stands, waiting for the majestic execution to happen.

'Kill him this time!'

'Don't let him go!'

'I love you, Prahlad!'

Amidst the clamour, Holika whispered, 'If it was up to me, I wouldn't do it.'

'But you did, just a few months back, dear aunt.'

'I was wrong. But you have hurt a lot of people and as you show no remorse or any desire to change, this has to be done,' she said. 'All I can say is, I wish I had more time to be with you.'

Prahlad nodded, feeling heavy-hearted as he was dragged into the arena. The elephant trumpeted, waving its trunk and stomping the ground. Five asura guards held it back so that it wouldn't run wild. The mahout sat atop the animal, making sure everything was in control.

A hush fell on the crowd as the master of ceremonies began in a loud, hoarse voice, 'Welcome people! We are here to witness the execution of our king's only remaining son, Prince Prahlad – the boy who went to the other side, betrayed his blood and joined hands with the terrorists. He's a warmonger and his hatred for our kind will only increase as time goes by if he's not put to death. He has murdered a minister and other officials in cold blood, attempted to decimate this city's economy and caused so much devastation that it pains my heart to continue. His father, our honourable king, is so filled with grief that he's not here. He's hurt – an emotion, I believe, all of us are feeling right now.'

And then the Asura looked at Prahlad, as if piercing his soul with his gaze. 'Now he shall face the wrath of his actions. Bring the elephant!'

Prahlad was pushed on to the block where the elephant's leg would crush him, breaking his bones and tearing his flesh. The elephant moved forward, loudly trumpeting as it came closer to him. He closed his eyes and began to chant Lord Vishnu's name and as the animal's shadow fell over him, he knew it was his definite end.

'O lord, help me,' he whispered a final plea as the elephant raised it's foot over his head.

All of a sudden, the crowd let out a collective gasp, and then there was silence. Confused, Prahlad waited. When he finally opened his eyes and turned towards the people, he saw they were gawking in surprise, not at him ... but someone else.

He looked up and was shocked to see the animal's foot suspended in mid-air, held aloft by a well-built man with a reddish beard.

His blood ran cold when he realized it was the same Simha, whom he was chatting with in the dungeon.

'Who are you?'

33
NARASIMHA

Flexing his muscles, Nara pushed the elephant. The animal began to lose its balance and toppled to the ground, the asura soldiers trapped beneath it. The roaring of the elephant mixed with the screams of the crowd and the soldiers, and in the ensuing chaos, Nara knew he had to escape with Prahlad.

'Can you open your binds?' he asked him.

Prahlad shook his head.

'Bah!' Nara grunted as he pulled Prahlad up, so he could at least walk, but noticed his legs were bound too.

This is not going to go well. Nara saw that the Asura guards had surrounded them.

Okay calm down, take a deep breath. Focus on how to escape.

His eyes darted to the chariot in the midst of the crowd. Hoisting Prahlad onto his shoulder, he began to sprint towards the chariot when an Asura blocked his path. Still clutching Prahlad with one arm, Nara rammed his fist into the Asura's chest, grabbed him by his armour and flipped him in a wide arc over his head. The Asura landed on top of the other guards who were chasing behind him.

He leapt into the chariot, threw Prahlad on the seat and tossed aside the charioteer. He took hold of the reins.

'Boy?' Nara yelled, as the horses galloped through the meandering streets of Kashyapuri, leaving behind the busy commotion, the fallen elephant and the confused Asura guards.

'Yes?' Prahlad asked, trying to gnaw through the ropes at his wrists.

'Be a friend and help me through these streets since you've practically lived your entire life here.'

He peered over the sides of the chariot to get his bearings. 'One of the ways to escape is from the wall which is under restoration since Indra's attack. It's being rebuilt. The other way is blocked because the last time, we had come from there and Holika had blocked it with extra measures,' he shouted out.

Following Prahlad's instructions, Nara sped through the streets, crashing through roadside shops and stalls, overturning carts full of produce and merchandise. Behind them, a legion of Asura soldiers gave chase on horseback.

Oh by the virtue of Lord Vishnu, save me, Prahlad thought in horror as they were ambushed by another troop of palace guards at the next turning.

Even as the guards let loose a volley of arrows, Nara whipped the horses into a frenzy and broke through the ranks of the guards, scattering them like leaves in the wind.

'Yes!' Nara yelled triumphantly, steering the chariot through the narrow lanes of Kashyapuri.

As they hurtled forward, he turned back to Prahlad. 'Are you sure this is the right way? There's just water in front.'

'Yeah, well, jump over it,' Prahlad said. 'That's the only way to get rid of them.'

'Are you mad, boy?'

'I haven't been tested!' Prahlad scowled.

'Okay, here we go.'

Nara sped up a ramp and urged the horses into jumping over the canal that ran through the city. Here and there armed Asura soldiers stood on rooftops, crossbows at the ready. An arrow pierced him in the back, but the pain was nothing compared to what he knew was coming. The restoration wall was barely a hundred yards away. Most of the bricks in the wall had been set in place, but were yet to be cemented together. There was no way the horses would go through the wall. The Asuras were close behind.

'I'm going to do something insane,' Nara said. 'What's beyond the wall?'

'A river that goes into the woods.'

'Great, I'm going to stop the horses now.'

'What?' Prahlad shrieked.

Taking the reins in one hand, Nara hauled Prahlad up to his side and held on to him. As soon as they neared the wall, he jerked the reins back forcefully, bringing the horses to a sudden halt. The impact threw the two of them out of the chariot and into the wall. Holding Prahlad tightly to his chest, Nara broke through the half-finished wall with his back. They landed on the other side of the wall, rolled on the ground and fell into the river.

And as the current carried them downstream, Nara tightened his hold on Prahlad and closed his eyes, relieved to have escaped.

Once the river entered the woods, Nara towed Prahlad to the bank, where he cut away his binds. He looked his reflection in the river and grimaced. He felt naked without his mane, as though he was not longer a Simha. It broke his heart.

'Thank you for saving me,' said Prahlad.

Nara smiled. This was the only silver lining.

'I am sure it wasn't my religious gibberish that inspired you to save me.' Prahlad chuckled.

'No, no, I um … I just thought … You seemed like a good person.'

'How did you escape?'

'I um … was helped by someone,' Nara said, smiling to himself.

'Hey, what's that?'

'What?'

'That.' Prahlad pointed at his chest.

Nara looked down and found it, a glinting symbol in the middle of his chest. His heart sank. He would have recognized the criss-cross symbol anywhere. It continued to glow until the mark had burned into his chest. It was the Shrivatsa symbol.

I have sealed my destiny.

'You are ... hold on ... I have read about this in Guru Narada's notes.' Prahlad eyed Nara, slowly touching his chest, 'You are ... you are an avatar?' He fell back. 'I was just saved by an avatar of Lord Vishnu. It's true! Lord Vishnu has saved me! It's true!'

Nara watched as his companion jumped and punched the air in delight. 'You don't understand the repercussions,' he said at last.

'What do you mean?'

'I shouldn't be the avatar. There shouldn't be an Avatar at all.'

'Why? They bring order and justice.'

'Not in this Yug.' Nara looked back at his reflection, recalling what Lord Rudra had told him, the *secret*. 'In this Yug, the avatar doesn't bring order.'

'Then?'

A grimace began to form on the Simha's face as he completed the sentence with a heavy heart. 'In this Yug, Prahlad, the avatar brings *chaos*.'

34
HOLIKA

The room felt stuffy, heavy with anger and fear. Hiranya sat at the table with a goblet in his hand. It had been a few hours since the mayhem at the arena.

Holika stood to one side, wary, watchful. She was secretly glad that Prahlad had escaped. She hadn't wanted to kill him. She hated him for what happened to Simhika, but perhaps time had healed her and allowed her to forgive him.

Andhaka was in the room too and Holika felt the hair on the nape of her neck rise whenever he turned towards her, sniffing. She didn't know if he could see her or not, but she got the impression that he could pierce through souls.

'Not only did my son escape but so did my wife's killer?' Hiranya thundered, gripping the silver goblet so hard in his hand that it broke, shattering into tiny pieces. 'Are they working together?'

'Seems like it,' murmured Andhaka.

'Andhaka? Did you notice who it was that released the Simha?'

'I have no clue, uncle.'

Hiranya shook his head, 'What will we do? We don't know where they are. The presence of Indra looms. My men tell me that Indra's son died when I attacked Naglok. He thinks I did it.'

'Yes,' Holika said, having heard about it from her spies. 'He's furious and we need to handle this before we go head on against him. As far as I've heard, Indra is collecting his army and plans to attack soon.'

'Give or take ten days,' added Andhaka. 'My riders say they are still far off and Indra is making a treaty with lesser known tribals for the great war.'

'Then we need to gather our men too.' Hiranya nodded.

'I have an idea, uncle,' Andhaka said stepping forward. 'I took the liberty of talking to the soldiers who were at the siege of Naglok, and I learnt that they had seen a Simha throwing Jayant from the chariot. Could it be the same Simha who escaped a few hours back?'

Hiranya stood up. 'There was no other Simha. Could this Narasimha have killed Jayant?'

'Even if he didn't, we can spread the word that he did, redirecting Indra's ire towards Nara.' Andhaka smiled.

'Good idea. Do that.' Hiranya turned to Holika. 'You are quiet, sister. What happened? You've always been enthusiastic about killing. Have you figured out how to take down the Vishnusena?'

Holika opened her mouth to speak, but the only images in her mind were of eight-year-old Prahlad strolling through the corridors of the great hall, and of herself, failing to pick him up when he fell down.

'Why don't we ask for a treaty?' Andhaka interrupted. 'The Vishnusena have changed their location since the last time I saw them. We can announce through villagers in the outskirts of Kashyapuri that we are seeking a treaty. Curiosity will compel them to respond. We lure them out, especially Prahlad and the old Narasimha to sign the treaty in a house of lac and wax, and burn the place down.'

'What about the other Vishnusena soldiers?' Holika asked.

'As a mole, I saw that Prahlad was the true leader of the group,' said Andhaka. 'If we cut the leader, there is no one else to follow.'

'But who will go?' Hiranya asked.

'Why you, uncle.'

There was a note of fear in Hiranya's voice. 'No, I still can't see my son die in front of me. Can't you go, Andhaka?'

'They'll not trust me. They'll think this ruse is some sort of a malicious plan,' he said.

'Then the only person left ...' Hiranya looked up at Holika.

She wanted to protest, malign him for wanting to kill his own child but not having the stomach to do it himself. She could see right through him. But he was the king and the king should be obeyed.

'Fine,' Holika said, 'let me know how this will work out.'

35

NARASIMHA

Lord Rudra was dying. Age had rendered him old and frail, no longer able to cling to his mortal form. He had called for Nara and the Simha leader had come at once. The room was dark and the only light came from the candle next to the bed.

'Nar …' Lord Rudra breathed in sharp, short breaths.

'My lord, I'm here.' Nara came forward and clasped Rudra's hand. 'What did you need me for?'

'I need to tell you something.'

'Yes, my lord.'

'You are so young.' Rudra chuckled. 'You have so much to learn.'

'Yes, my lord.'

'I don't know how long I have and I have kept a secret that you should know. It concerns you. I sense you are acquiring the powers of Dharm.'

Nara nodded. He had been more powerful than other Simhas, tougher and faster. Lord Indra did remark that that he would be a Dharm, on the way to becoming the next avatar.

'Yes, my lord.'

'Do not let the vanity of the title get to you. The obscure truth of this yug is something not many know. The thing is, in this yug, the avatar is the one who wreaks havoc.'

'But doesn't the avatar save the world?'

'Not in this yug, no.' Rudra paused as he was seized by a bout of coughing. 'He's the one who brings the worst kind of casualties. You have to make sure, Nara, that you don't let yourself be the avatar.'

'But how will I do that?'

'Leave. Run. Do not let destiny trick you into becoming one.' He coughed again. 'It also said something else.'

'What?'

Lord Rudra looked at Nara with pale blue eyes so deep and sad that Nara shivered. 'That the avatar loses to Adharm in this yug.'

Nara listened in disbelief. *The Avatar lose to* Adharm? *Impossible!* He wondered if Lord Rudra had become delusional in his final moments.

Nara gazed at the shimmering sunset, whose orange rays hit his face. He could hear the humdrum of the Vishnusena camp behind him. He had made Prahlad promise not to tell them that he was an avatar, even though the boy had said that it would make him their leader.

But I don't want to be the leader, he thought.

'Nara?' A familiar voice came from behind him.

Nara turned to see Prahlad, who came and sat next to him. 'How do you feel?'

'I'm okay,' said Nara. And physically, he was. The symbol had just shown up and hadn't made much of a difference to his overall physiology. Mentally, emotionally – now that was another matter.

'You should tell them,' he said.

'You can't convince me. Do you not realize the repercussions of what has just happened?'

'You know,' Prahlad said, 'when I look back, I remember what my guruji had told me. What you do is a result of your choice, and what destiny wants you to do, it is the will of Lord Vishnu. And no one can overturn Lord Vishnu's will. I always used to worry that I can't break destiny, this chakravyuh, but I think I was wrong now.'

'Why so?'

'I feel if a man is right and he's out there doing the righteous thing, he will break this will and Lord Vishnu himself will bless him for doing the right thing. No destiny can stop him.'

'Look, a fourteen-year-old teaching me about life!' Nara rolled his eyes. 'What a moment!'

'Sarcastic, I see.' Prahlad chuckled. 'Life is all about breaking away from what is destined for you and doing things such that the gods themselves bow down and say he's a man of his own actions.' He paused. 'I know what you have learnt about the symbol, but if you complete your karma and continue to be a good man, I don't think that'll happen.'

'But I'm not a good man,' he said images of Anuhrad, Kayadhu and all the people he had killed flashed before his eyes. 'I don't think I ever was. Also, I have this anger.'

'What is it?'

'When I'm angry, I lose myself. I let my anger control me. I take deep breaths to hold it, but that doesn't always work. Although nothing quite triggers open this jar of snakes like one person.'

'Who is that?'

'Her name is Chenchen. I really love her. Even though she was supposed to come with me here, I knew she would be my weakness and I'd lose control. But I can't let that happen.'

'I understand. A woman, right? I like a girl too.' Prahlad winked. 'She's uh ... never mind.'

'No, come on, tell me,' Nara urged him.

'No, I mean I don't know if it's interesting enough.'

'Of course it is, boy. Tell me.'

Prahlad blushed. 'There's a girl here. Dhriti. I really like her.'

'That's good. She likes you back?'

'Yeah, she does.'

'It's a privilege to be loved back by the person you love. Not many have that.' Nara smiled.

Prahlad sighed. 'It feels good to share my feelings with someone.'

'Well,' Nara said, patting him on the back, 'I'm always here, boy. Remember that. I'm here to ...' *Protect you, serve you* – Nara didn't know what to say. 'I need to tell you something.'

'Yes?'

Nara had just coughed up the courage to speak about Anuhrad's and Kayadhu's deaths when he heard a sound. Screams from the camp about a visitor.

'There's a visitor!' Prahlad exclaimed, standing up. 'We must go. Not many know of this location, so I wonder how they knew of this.'

Nara followed Prahlad, myriad thought tumbling about in his head as he walked towards the centre of the camp where a group of people were on horseback, some men, but mostly women.

'It's the Matrikas!' shrieked Asamanja, the disputed leader of Vishnusena that Prahlad had introduced to Nara. 'My lady, what are you doing here and how did you know of this place?'

It was obvious that Asa was elated to see the Matrikas, who wouldn't be a part of any war without a certain price. They supported those who had the money and food to pay them. And Nara knew that Asa would want to hire them for their help against the city's monarch.

The woman in the middle, wearing golden armour and carrying a noose, dismounted from her horse. 'We come in peace. I seek to know something, chief. Perhaps we could speak inside your tent.'

'Yes, my lady. Please come in.' Asamanja guided the woman inside. As the other Matrikas dismounted, Nara's eyes fell on one of the women. She looked familiar. Quite familiar. 'Chenchen!' he yelled.

The women turned. She looked different in her armour and with a weapon. She looked so … rough and beautiful. Her eyes widened. All the Matrikas stopped to see what was happening and even the members of the Vishnusena seemed curious.

And then Chenchen was running towards him as fast as she could. Nara held out his arms and she embraced him with all her strength. He wrapped his arms around her , letting the familiar smell of lavender envelop him.

She looked up and smiled, 'You are here. You can't … How?'

Nara didn't say anything. He just kissed her. And after a long time, he felt harmony, peace and, most importantly, hope seep into his soul.

36

HOLIKA

The days following the meeting were tough. Holika had been prepping her army for any sort of problem or a surprise attack. The restoration of the walls was complete. Catapults were stationed on the outskirts of the city. Security had been increased and while much of the Asura army was stationed at Naglok and Yakshlok, Kashyapuri held the largest number of the soldiers since it was the capital and Indra's focal point of attack.

Holika was just glad that Asuras ruled most of Illavarti now. The only place left was Devlok, which perhaps Hiranya was in no mood to conquer. He was exhausted from the petty war he was having with the Vishnusena. Holika had formed a few reconnaissance groups that would disguise themselves and go in the outskirts, searching for their camp. She wanted to find the rebel army before Andhaka put his terrible plan in motion.

She didn't want Prahlad to get hurt. She couldn't bring him back because now, even his own father hated him. She didn't know what she wanted from him or how she would rescue him, but it would not be like this.

Holika was in her office, reading the last part of Prahlad's journal. She just hoped the insolent boy would understand the empire he was fighting against. The only way to defeat Hiranya was to kill him, which would result in a leadership vacuum. But to kill Hiranya, was a task in itself. He was invincible.

She looked at the journal and read the part where she was last mentioned.

One of the moments with Aunt Holika I clearly remember is the time when her roars were heard all over the palace.

I was nine then and confused as to what could be the reason behind such commotion. Just like the handmaidens and the guards, I walked down the corridor to where my aunt, red-faced with anger, was shouting that a sword from her priceless twin pair was missing.

There weren't any clues as to where it had gone, but of course the sword didn't have any feet of its own on which it might have scurried had away. She blamed everyone from the priests to the guards to her servants. I found out that she had sent the swords for sharpening at the blacksmith but only one of them returned.

I was a curious kid. I realized that if I found her sword, it would overshadow whatever anger she had towards me. I rushed around the palace, hoping to find it. I retraced the sword's steps from the blacksmith to the palace, meeting my friend Viparichit who told me that the two swords were taken away from that shop for sure.

I finally found it in a corner where it had been accidentally left behind by the person who was supposed to bring it to court. I picked it up with a grin and went knocking at her door.

The moment she saw the sword, she snatched it away.

'How dare you!' she sneered.

My smile vanished. 'No, I found it for you, Aunty.'

'You stole it, you stupid, reckless boy.'

'No, I didn't.' I was pale and confused.

'Don't ever touch my things or I shall hurt you,' she growled and shut the door in my face.

I kept standing there, confused, and horrified. I was hurt. I couldn't deal with it any more. I was exhausted from trying to get her approval and it was time for me to not care any more. I believe one shouldn't have to seek approval if they are on the right side.

And from then on, whenever it came to Aunt Holika, I neither spoke nor intervened in her matters. She never behaved like my aunt, and so I stopped acting like her nephew.

Holika put the journal away. She remembered the incident clearly and how she had regretted it the instant she had got angry on the little boy. Then, she had dismissed the thought and continued living her life, never realizing the impact it had had on him. There was a knock on the door and she opened it to Andhaka.

'Yes?' she grunted.

'Hope you are not busy.'

'No. Please tell me what it is.'

'I am executing our plan. I have sent the message to everyone in the villages that we seek peace with the Vishnusena and that if they want, they should meet us in the house east of the river, five hundred yards away from Kashyapuri, seven days from now. We have promised to send only one official, and no army, to show our willingness to listen to their terms and negotiate.'

'Do you think they will come?'

'They are desperate. I know they'll come,' Andhaka said with absolute certainty. 'And if they don't, I'll scout them and kill them all. But that will take a lot of time that I don't have.'

'Yes, I agree.' Holika nodded glumly. 'Is that it? Anything else?'

Andhaka clapped and a man with a bushy moustache entered, holding a long coat.

'I had a costume specially designed for you.'

The man showed the hood of the coat which could be wrapped around her entire body. 'It's made of wool and modacrylic fire retardants.'

'What do you expect me to do with it?' Holika arched her brows.

'It'll help you escape unscathed when we burn down the rendezvous location,' said Andhaka.

Holika touched the coat, feeling the thick fabric. 'Are you sure it will work?'

'Of course, we have tried it, my lady.'

Holika wore the coat with the help of Andhaka who seemed to be strangely capable, considering he couldn't see.

'You'll be safe when you do the deed.' Andhaka smiled triumphantly, patting her on the shoulder. 'My lady, I hope you realize, you are doing a great thing, right?'

Holika nodded. 'Thank you, Andhaka.'

She could sense the malice behind his winsome smile. She had no doubt he was a genius, and had a sinister, diabolical plan that perhaps only he knew of. What remained to be seen was if he was really a loyal servant of the empire or something else.

37

CHENCHEN

The moment was finally here, and all she could do was gaze into his eyes. She never realized that all the tiny steps she had taken would bring her here, right to his arms and his beautiful, warm smile.

They were in the woods, away from prying eyes as they held on to each other. The Matrikas were with the Vishnusena, but she didn't care what they talked about, for she was here with Nara.

'You look different,' he smiled.

'You too. You don't have your ...'

'I lost it,' he admitted sadly.

And he told her everything, right from when he had left the Shiva fortress in the hills. They sat amongst the tulips where the light was dim. After hearing his story, Chenchen hugged him again. 'You are safe and that's what matters.'

'I know,' he said, tightening his arms around her. 'What happened to you?'

'Oh, don't ask.'

She too told him her tale from the beginning.

'I had no purpose there. There was nothing holding me back any more. I knew I wanted to do something more than just heal people. I wanted to save the world.'

'Why this sudden urge?'

'I don't know – seeing you made me realize it.' She looked down at his chest where she noticed something, glinting behind the shawl he wore. She pushed the shawl off his chest and she saw the Shrivatsa symbol, the one he had spoken about earlier. 'You have it. But … '

'I know,' he said, shaking his head, 'I'm nervous.'

'Don't be. It'll work out, I'm sure.'

'Seeing you made me realize how much I was missing my other life.' Nara smiled. 'The life where I could have been with you.'

'What you chose and what you follow is the truest path you can be on.' Chenchen gazed into his eyes and smiled. 'I'm proud of you.'

'But I might create chaos or kill someone or do what Lord Rudra –'

Chenchen put her finger on his lips. 'It's okay, calm down. Everything will be okay.'

She glanced at the shawl. 'You are trying to conceal the fact that you are an avatar, aren't you?'

He nodded.

'Why?'

'Because I don't want to give people hope that I might save them.' Nara sighed. 'I can't deal with the pressure.'

'You saved Prahlad, right?'

Nara didn't say anything.

'Embrace yourself, your destiny and what you are made for,' Chenchen said. 'You were on the right track after the Andhaka episode. What happened?'

'This symbol made me rethink things. I'm scared.'

'We all are,' she said, 'and that's why we have been brought here together, to support each other. Trust that everything will fall into place.'

They hugged each other for a long while, letting the silence comfort them. His hands laced across her back, playing with the ends of her hair. The warmth settled between them and he felt ... at home.

When Chenchen entered the main tent of the Vishnusena chief, she heard Brahmani saying, 'That's why we are here. We need your help to find Andhaka.'

Asamanja, the chief, looked surprised and interested. 'I'm surprised that the Matrikas seek our assistance when it should have been the other way around.'

'The goddess Nrriti guided us here,' Chamunda said. 'We thought Skanda ... Andhaka would be here but he's not.'

'He *was* until he betrayed us,' Prahlad, the black-haired, ivory-skinned boy said bitterly. 'Believe me, he's not worth the trouble. He's malicious –'

'He might be,' Parvati snapped, interrupting the boy, 'but he's also important. We need him.'

Chenchen realized that the Matrikas hadn't revealed that Andhaka was Parvati's son and that he was the prophetic saviour. But then logically speaking, why would they?

'Well, my ladies, I am not so sure how to find him, to be honest,' Asa said, with a grimace. 'But you are welcome to stay here while we come up with a plan together to find him.'

'We don't have time,' Brahmani announced. 'You said he was in Kashyapuri? Can we somehow lure him out?'

'There is a way.'

The occupants of the tent turned towards to the opening to see who had spoken.

Nara emerged from the darkness outside and walked over to Chenchen's side. 'I know more about Andhaka than anyone here because ... I killed him once.'

Everyone gasped and Parvati clenched her jaw. She knew Nara. But she didn't hate him for his reasons were valid.

'Andhaka takes in orphans and makes them go through a process of becoming his other selves,' Nara said. 'We can send a Vishnusena soldier who fits the profile to the village, someone Andhaka might want to take in. And when he comes to collect our "orphan", we can nab him.'

'Who will fit the profile?' Brahmani asked.

'Well, a bald kid or a man, someone who's pale.'

Asa spoke up: 'I have someone. He can be the bait. But how will we know where in the village to send him so he can lure Andhaka out?'

'It's easy,' Nara said, 'I know his smell and we can find him, placing the decoy there.'

Seeing the uncertain faces around him, he added, 'I know it's a long shot, but this is our only chance. We don't have the manpower to launch a full-scale attack on Kashyapuri. The security on the palace has been doubled since Prahlad and I escaped, which makes sneaking in and out nearly impossible.'

'I know it's a long shot but this is our only chance. Attacking the city is stupid since it's too difficult to enter or exit the place, especially since me.

Brahmani looked at Asa. 'Will you help us, chief?'

'Of course, my lady! You are after all the great Matrikas. I would love to get my vengeance on Andhaka who has betrayed and outsmarted us. It'll be good to outsmart him for once.' Asa smiled.

Another person entered the tent just then, her red hair making her stand out.

'We have some important news,' she said.

'What is it, Dhriti?' Prahlad asked.

The girl looked at everyone licked her lips before she spoke. 'The Asura empire wants a treaty with us.'

38

PRAHLAD

They walked to the house mentioned in the message. Prahlad, Asa and Dhriti had their hoods on and kept a close watch on the house. It was deserted and Asa wanted to make sure the treaty wasn't a trap with soldiers waiting to apprehend them. When they scanned the area and found no one, they went to the house – a broken shack with red walls and a straw roof.

'So this is it,' Asa announced.

The treaty specified the time and the day and the venue but didn't go into specifics about the truce. One of the Vishnusena soldiers had seen the notices posted all the over every village and brought one back.

'Seems all right,' Dhriti remarked. 'Nothing too spectacular about it.'

'Makes you wonder why they chose this place,' Prahlad said.

'Probably because it's obscure, far enough from the city so we wouldn't feel we are under attack,' Dhriti suggested. It sounded logical but something was amiss about this entire scenario. She said, 'Why did they want a truce all of a sudden? It just doesn't make sense.'

Asa responded instantly, 'We don't have a choice, do we? We have to go with what we are given. At least, let's hear them out.'

Prahlad wanted to protest that the last time they had heard Andhaka out, things hadn't gone according to plan. He had gone against them and everything had spiralled out of control.

'I think if we station our men,' Asa said, pointing to the hills, 'on each end, concealed under the canopies, we will have good backup. This is only if the Asuras are trying to trick us.'

'Why would they want a truce? Have you honestly thought about it?' Prahlad asked.

'Probably because they can't find us and that is the one advantage we have over them,' Asa replied. 'They might be a superpower, but we are like rats, hiding in nooks and crannies.'

'And this is their way to lure us out,' Prahlad said. 'Let me go inside alone.'

'Are you mad? I'm the chief of Vishnusena,' Asa said, gritting his teeth, his dreadlocks falling over his forehead. 'I have to be there. *You* don't. You are a kid, Prahlad. I am glad you believe in our cause, but after the last problem where you got caught and were about to die ... We just can't lose you.'

'He's right,' Dhriti added.

Prahlad remembered how Dhriti had hugged him once he came back and how nice it had felt. She had cried, saying that she had wanted to help him. They hadn't thought he would be executed since he was from royal blood.

'I thought you were immune to their attacks,' Dhriti said. 'But you're not. You are staying at the camp now.'

Prahlad shook his head. 'You can't keep me from coming here. When I joined the Vishnusena, I knew the risks and I still did it. So you can't stop me.'

He looked at Asa and said, 'I'll be here when the treaty is being discussed. I will know what they might be doing, fooling around in the city since I've ruled the damn city. Andhaka caught me by surprise, because I was never close to him. I will never make that mistake again.'

'Well, for Andhaka, we are all to blame.' Asa sighed. 'Fine, you can come. But if they launch an attack, you leave. All right? You won't stay back.'

Prahlad knew he would stay even if he was on the verge of death, but he nodded to pacify them. He looked at Dhriti but she ignored him. Clearly, she was unhappy with this plan. But he couldn't let that affect his decision. He knew he was a part of something bigger than him, than all of them.

He only hoped the treaty wasn't a hoax.

39

NARASIMHA

The night was dense and Nara could hear the hooting of the owl from afar. They were all in disguise. Nara had drawn a hood over his mane, which he had acquired recently. He was in the corner, while on the other side, he could see Chenchen and Brahmani. On his right was Chamunda.

'I hope he comes tonight,' she said.

'He's supposed to. Once I sniffed his scent, I asked around this village and they confirmed that they had seen a bald man with a red bandanna,' Nara replied. 'He comes here often and he takes people with him, sometimes in the guise of paying them or granting glory and fame.'

He saw the decoy beggars that the Matrikas had stationed. They were all kids belonging to the Vishnusena; some of them were bald, while others had thick locks of hair.

'We have waited for a few days now,' Nara added, reminding himself that today was also the day the treaty was supposed to be discussed. 'Seven days exactly.'

'And every day was a failed attempt,' Chamunda reminded him. 'I hope today isn't one. Your plan, if it doesn't work, will create issues for us because then we'll have to think of an alternative.'

Nara grudgingly nodded, recalling the conversation he had had with Chenchen a few days ago.

'I should be the one to apprehend him. And I am not going to let the Matrikas think they can have him. He's mine. He killed Bhairav. I need to have his head.'

'You don't understand.' Chenchen held his arm. They were in his tent. 'Andhaka is not who he says he is. He thinks he knows it all, but he doesn't. He's Skanda, the son of Shiva and Parvati, the protector of mankind.'

'But he's evil,' Nara said tightly. 'He wants mayhem. How can he be a protector?'

'He's not evil, Nara. There's more to him, you know that. I told you about his past. You know how challenging his past was. I think he can really change,' she said softly.

'You're being idealistic.' Nara shook his head. They heard someone outside the hut. 'Who is it?'

A mane-wearing woman entered; Nara instantly recognized her as a Simhi.

'I'm Pratyangira.' She smiled.

Nara nodded. 'How can I help you, my lady?'

'I noticed you don't have your mane.'

'Yes, I lost it,' he said, looking at his claws. They were growing, and he was glad about it.

'If you don't mind,' Pratyangira offered, glancing at Chenchen as though seeking approval, 'I have a friend's mane with me, if you want.'

'Friend? A Simha's skin is most important. How did he leave it with you?'

'He died, a long time back. I have held on to it, but I thought you might want it when I saw you.' Pratyangira added, drawing it out from her bag.

'Um …' Nara contemplated, stealing a glance at Chenchen who was clearly annoyed; she didn't like it when he received female attention, but seemed to be holding her tongue at the moment. 'Sure, that's very kind of you.'

The Simhi nodded and left, leaving the mane behind.

'She's just being nice, Chenchen.' Nara chuckled.

as Chenchen rolled her eyes and pulled a face.

'On a serious note,' Nara began, 'I hope you will let me have Andhaka and not the Matrikas. Don't stop me.'

'I don't know.' She paused thoughtfully. 'I was with them for a while, and they have been really nice to me … I just …'

'Take some time to think about this,' Nara said. 'But I would really like it if you supported me.'

He didn't say any more, proceeding instead to wear the mane, the skin which had belonged to someone else, and yet made him feel better than he had in the days since he lost his own.

He waited under the cover of darkness with the others, whistling to himself. It had been a while since he had actually rested. His body was flaming up and being shaken up by searing jolts of pain. But he knew he wanted to kill Andhaka – if he found the right one. Anuhrad's advice hadn't borne fruit, but he also knew that when he found the next Andhaka, he would check if he was blind or not, just like he had checked last time. And he would have the highest probability of killing him, even though it would be a risk. He should have killed the Andhaka who opened the cell for him, but he had felt too grateful then.

Why am I regretting it now?

Because that Andhaka might have been fake. He could have been innocent.

But anyone associated with Andhaka cannot be innocent and I should realize that.

'You know,' Chamunda began, 'you said there are many Andhakas. will we know if the one who comes is the real one?'

Nara clenched his jaw. 'You won't. But as far as I know, if I want to get a duplicate of myself, I will go there myself to choose.'

'It does make sense but …'

'He's always one step ahead of us,' Nara completed her thought and Chamunda glanced at him worriedly.

'I used to have one of those,' he said, pointing at the trident she was carrying.

'What happened to it?'

'I lost it,' Nara admitted regretfully. 'I don't know where it is now. But anyway.'

Before he could say anything else, he heard the clatter of hooves and a chariot barging through the middle of the streets of the silent village. From the carriage, came a wiry man. He would bear an uncanny resemblance to a skeleton if it wasn't for his red bandanna.

'It's him,' Nara confirmed grimly, before coming out of the shadows.

40

PRAHLAD

It was *the* night. Prahlad waited outside the red hut along with Asa, who was decked in armour. Before long, a woman emerged from the shadows, a soldier on either side holding torches in their hands and no weapons.

No weapon? Strange, thought Prahlad.

Asa and Prahlad glanced at each other in confusion. They had expected more people to come.

Holika stood opposite them and the deathly silence was broken by Asa whispering to Prahlad, 'Best of luck.'

'I'm glad you are here,' Holika said to Prahlad, who nodded in return.

'We are surprised, my lady, that you come into this abandoned place with no army.'

'We are here to discuss a truce, are we not?' Holika shrugged. 'I bear no anger towards you. The palace has appointed me to deal with you. I want you to trust me and my word, thus I am making myself vulnerable, even though your men may be hiding nearby, waiting to capture me for ransom or—'

'We want peace as much as you do. I am Asamanja, leader of the Vishnusena.'

Holika nodded, and led the way into the hut while the soldiers remained outside. Prahlad notice her strange bulky coat, but he did not comment on it. Asa said, 'Tell me, my lady, how can we reach this settlement?'

'What are your demands?'

'Dismantle the reign of the Asura king, Hiranyakashyap,' Asa said placidly. 'That man caused the deaths of my wife and children. His men raped her and threw her away like she was garbage. I demand justice.'

'He can't leave the grounds, Chief,' Holika flared her nostrils, 'It's not how it works. We can work out a different arrangement. Otherwise we will have to involve the citizens of Hiranyapur.'

A cold shiver swept through Prahlad's body as he thought of the big city of danavs – brothers to the Asuras.

'We have not summoned them yet and when we do, it won't be pretty. It's best if you abandon this demand before we have to call them.'

'We will keep hiding till you lose your resources.' Asa smiled. 'The Danavs are scary but also boorish and indulgent. If Hiranyakashyap cannot step down, then I have another demand – bring up idol worshipping, especially that of Lord Vishnu in all the holy places of Kashyapuri and rename the city Manavpur, what it used to be called.

There was a pause. Prahlad watched her consider this.

'And grant us immunity against any surprise attacks or prosecution by your government,' Asa added.

Holika nodded. 'I suppose it's fair but I'll have to discuss this with the king.' She looked at Prahlad. 'Can I talk to my nephew alone?'

Asa nodded and left the hut. Prahlad and Holika stared at each other silently.

'I just wanted to say,' Holika began, 'I am sorry for everything, for how I treated you. I know I have not been a good aunt, in fact I have not been a good person. But I feel, everyone should be given a second chance. Do you forgive me?'

'Why do you say that?'

'I read your journal.'

Prahlad froze. The idea of his personal belongings in the hands of his aunt made his skin crawl, but he was surprised by Holika's words. 'Um, I accept your apology,' he mumbled.

'If it wasn't for my disdain, would you still have been a follower of this Vishnusena?' she asked, her voice gentler than he ever remembered.

'Being here, with them,' Prahlad said, 'had nothing to do with you. You did ignore me all my life, but I never hated you. Not even on the day when you wanted to kill me.'

Holika nodded and her eyes were misty. 'I am sorry … I have been a horrible woman.' She took off her coat and gave it to him. 'Wear this.'

'Why?'

'Just wear it.'

That's when Prahlad noticed the flames that were leaping across the walls towards the straw roof. The hut would be burn to the ground within minutes.

'What is going on!' he cried out. 'This was a trick after all,' he shouted, looking accusingly at his aunt.

'It's Andhaka and your father.' Holika still had the coat and ignoring his shouts, she grabbed him and made him wear it forcibly. 'It was all a plan. Your men stationed around have been apprehended and Asamanja is probably lying unconscious outside, all because of me. We are both locked inside.'

It began growing hotter and crackling orange flames bellowed like the insides of a creature.

'This coat was supposed to protect me.' Holika cupped his face in her palms. 'Only one of us can live through this.'

'But … but what about you?'

She leaned forward and whispered the secret of his father's newfound strength and the only way to defeat him.

'I don't want him to kill you, so I'm telling you this,' she said. 'Take care, my boy.'

He couldn't believe that Holika was sobbing. She was not the woman he had known her to be.

'I have not been a good aunt your entire life,' she said, ignoring the burning straw that was falling around them. 'Let me be that to you – just once.'

She pushed him hard and he fell back against the wall of the hut, breaking through it as the rest of the structure fell down on Holika. The last image of her, smiling with tears on her cheeks, standing in the heart of an inferno, would be burned in his mind forever.

41

NARASIMHA

Nara knew he would have only seconds to do it. He pulled his hood away and rushed towards Andhaka. His body flamed with energy and his claws shone in the moonlight as he chased him, only to realize the Matrikas, led by Brahmani, had reached him faster.

Andhaka, realizing something was wrong, tapped on his chariot. Nara paused and so did the Matrikas. Eleven Andhakas stood before them in a circle, and no one knew who the real one was.

'You can't catch me,' one of them said.

'It is impossible,' another said.

Nara came forward. 'Do you remember me?'

All the Andhakas turned to Nara, sniffing. 'Ah, if it isn't the Simha I have dealt with already,' one of them said, chuckling, while another gave a loud, insane laugh.

Trident in hand, Chamunda stood beside Nara, ready to attack. She said in a low voice, 'I think the one in the middle is Andhaka.'

The Andhakas instantly split, half of them confronting the Matrikas and the other half heading towards Nara. As the bald men came forward, wielding swords, Nara clawed out their torsos, and tossed them away. One jumped on top of him but he threw him across the pavement. Chamunda fought alongside him, doling out kicks and punches, trying to avoid killing an innocent Andhaka. It was getting tougher.

As Nara deflected the sword attack and punched an Andhaka, he turned and saw Chenchen on the ground, being choked by an Andhaka. He instantly ran towards her and with his shoulders, shoved the Andhaka to the side.

'Look out!' Chenchen yelled.

Nara glanced up just in time to dodge the blade slicing through the air towards him. A swift kick took care of the Andhaka approaching him from the back.

'This is not going well,' Nara said, helping Chenchen to her feet.

She pointed at a corner. 'There's a shadow. Someone is running away from the scuffle.'

Nara used his vision to clearly see that it was an Andhaka running towards the tulip field adjacent to the village.

Why is he running?

Nara grinned. 'Don't tell the Matrikas that he's gone that side. Let me finish this once and for all.'

Chenchen didn't say anything as Nara sprinted after the Andhaka. He ran through the tulip beds, his heart pounding as he closed the gap between him and the Andhaka. He went for his leg, scratching it hard – the flesh tore off and Andhaka fell on the ground.

Towering over the blind man, Nara growled, 'You can't get away from me now.'

'Don't … don't … please … I beg you …' Andhaka whimpered and this was the first time Nara had seen him anything but confident.

'You are the real one,' he smiled and brought his claws close to his throat, ready to do the deed.

'Leave him!' he heard a shout. Nara turned towards the voice and saw a woman a few yards away holding a bow and an arrow. It was Parvati.

'What are you doing?' Nara asked, wondering whether it was Chenchen who sent her in this direction. 'We finally got him.'

'I saw you run here,' Parvati said. 'It made me wonder why a warrior like you would desert us like this. Let Andhaka go!'

'What are you going to do with him?' Nara asked.

'Take him back. He's important to us.'

'It's because he's your son, isn't it?'

Parvati remained stiff, with the arrow pointing at him.

'Are you going to hurt me?' Nara chuckled. 'An arrow won't hurt me, my lady.'

'But an arrow in your eye can be quite troublesome. I don't miss. He's mine, Nara. Leave him,' Parvati ordered.

Nara, flaring his nostrils, turned back and moved away from Andhaka, who was still shivering on the ground. That was when Nara noticed two other Andhakas at the edge of the field. Before Nara could warn her, they had stabbed Parvati in the back. She collapsed on the field, as Nara ran towards them. He didn't care about not hurting them any more. He respected Lady Parvati as he had Lord Bhairav.

With mounting anger, he roared and grabbed the Andhakas by the throat. They flailed and clawed at his hands, but he was too powerful for them. He choked them and tossed their limp bodies aside.

'Please don't kill him,' Parvati coughed.

Nara closed his eyes, letting his bitter anger calm down; it was replaced by instant regret. But he cast it aside for now, as he looked back to where the real Andhaka was. Only, he wasn't there.

'He escaped,' Nara stamped his feet, 'Damn it!'

He looked at Parvati and picked her up in his arms. 'My lady, I apologize, I hope you are fine.'

Parvati held on to him and nodded. 'You were trying to kill my son, Nara. I had to stop you.'

'My lady, may I say something?' he asked as he carried her back to the village.

'Yes?'

'He's not your son any more,' Nara said. 'He's a degenerate and he murdered your husband.'

Parvati clenched her jaw, refusing to answer. They were two people with different ideologies. And in silence, they found a commonality – failure.

42

PRAHLAD

He staggered to his feet, behind him the burning rubble under which his aunt's body lay. All around him bows sang, arrows whooshed and sword clanged. Prahlad's world seemed to have narrowed down to this battlefield. He gulped and noticed someone running towards him. It was a man.

He dodged the spear the guard had thrust at him and hurled himself onto the man's chest, pushing him down on the ground and punching him until the guard was rendered unconscious.

I need to leave this place.

Prahlad began to walk through the smoke that had built up all around him. He rubbed his eyes, to see what was ahead of him, but he stumbled and fell. Confused and disoriented, he looked back, and let out a blood-curdling scream. Asa's lifeless body lay on the ground, watching him with blank eyes. His head had been smashed in, perhaps with a hammer.

No. No. No.

He gathered Asa in his arms. 'Wake up, brother. Wake up.'

As the smoke cleared he saw how the Vishnusena battling the Asura soldiers up in the hills. Amidst the fire and catapults, bodies lay everywhere; even in the darkness the earth gleamed blood-red. Prahlad began to drag Asa's corpse towards the forest, which seemed the only safe option. Suddenly he was confronted by a pair of Asura soldiers.

'The traitor!' One of them thrust his sword forward. Unarmed as he was, Prahlad raised his arm to stay the blade. It slashed through the woollen coat his aunt had given him.

'You killed Lady Holika!' the other asura bellowed. 'You tricked her!'

Prahlad had no way out. He was still holding on to Asa's corpse. The moment the soldier came closer, Prahlad dodged his attack and headbutted him. The soldier fell back groaning. Another sword slashed at Prahlad's back but the coat protected him. He grabbed the fallen soldier's weapon and stabbed the other Asura right under his arm.

Two more Asuras joined the fray. Still holding on to Asa's hand, Prahlad scanned his surroundings for an escape route. And just then, arrows bolted right through one Asura. He fell down, and another zapped through the second one, who collapsed.

He turned in the direction the arrows had come from, he saw Dhriti. She ran up to him and hugged him quickly. She looked at Asa's corpse and gasped.

'You must leave him if we are to survive,' she said, her voice strong but eyes filled with tears.

'I can't. It's … it's my fault.'

'No, it's not.' She pressed her palms against his cheeks. 'Let's go. We were ambushed and I told my men to scatter. We can't fight them, not for long.'

'Holika ... Holika sacrificed,' Prahlad said, his voice now a weak quiver.

'What happened?'

'It was planned. The treaty, they don't want – '

'It's okay,' she said and pulled him into the forest.

Away from the mayhem. Away from the darkness. As he ran away from everything, his mind darted towards two things – Asa's corpse and Holika's sacrifice.

He wanted to avenge his friend. And he wanted to do right by his aunt.

43

HIRANYAKASHYAP

She was dead. But he didn't mourn for her, for it took him more than few days to accept the fact that his loving sister was gone, her body nothing but ash. And the worst part? It was his son who was responsible. Or that's what his men said.

Hiranya rammed his fist into the shield of the soldier nearest to him. The pain jarred through his body, momentarily distracting him from his grief. He was in his training arena, surrounded by soldiers holding up shields that he would punch. One after another, he smashed the shields into pieces, hurling the last one across the arena angrily. He slumped to his knees with a cry of frustration and punched the ground. The earth shook.

His Brahmshastra glowed in the light, splitting the orange rays into many.

He saw a strange, thin man with papery hair enter the arena. Hirnaya recognized him immediately. It was Kalanemi, Andhaka's creepy assistant.

Hiranya halted his practice and looked at the assistant. 'What do you want?'

'It's Lord Andhaka who sent me, master.' Kalanemi bowed. He had a way of not speaking with his teeth, or perhaps he didn't have teeth.

'How is he now?'

The last time Hiranya had seen Andhaka, he was scarred and nursing a huge gash on his leg – claw marks courtesy of the Simha.

'Still healing, my lord. It has come to our attention that word has spread about Lady Holika's actions for her nephew.' Kalanemi directed one of the soldiers to come forward. He was carrying a synthetic cloth depicting an obese, hideous woman with a large nose about to burn a child in a cauldron. 'They are saying that Lady Holika tried killing him by burning him on her lap, but he was protected by Lord Vishnu and he survived. The day this happened has been marked by your people as a victory of good over evil.'

'Who did this?' Hiranya grimaced, grabbing the painting and instantly tearing it apart.

'We have imprisoned him, my lord,' Kalanemi said. 'A Vishnu sympathizer. The people apparently believe he's *really* protected by Lord Vishnu and since there are more Manavs here than Asuras, they all are planning to revolt against you and bring back the old city.'

Hiranya had been afraid of this. He couldn't kill civilians, not his people. But then, were they his people if they revolted against him?

'Listen,' Hiranya began.

Kalanemi's eyes went wide with absolute delight as Hiranya continued, 'Find the other sympathizers who are revolting or secretly inciting rebellion. I want them all impaled.' Hiranya ordered his men loudly, 'There will be no reward for insolence in my state. Understood?'

Everyone nodded.

Hiranya looked at Kalanemi, his eyes narrowing with disgust. 'Take me to the painter.'

Hiranya stalked across the dungeon with Kalanemi staggering after him. The prisoners cowered in their cells, terrified of invoking the wrath of the Asura king. When they reached the cell which was their destination, Hiranya stood aside while Kalanemi fumbled with the keys for a bit before finally pushing open the door. The occupant of the cell shrank against the wall at the far end as Hiranya entered.

'Did you do this?' the Asura king asked, showing the painter the torn pieces of the painting.

The painter didn't say anything. Instead, he began to chant under his breath.

'Oh,' Hiranya chuckled, 'Are you worshipping your god? It's nice. Do that. I'll wait.'

The painter joined his hands and chanted louder. 'He shall get you,' he rasped, finally opening his eyes, 'and you shall face Lord Vishnu's wrath soon, by the hands of your son.'

Hiranya grit his teeth. 'I'm waiting for your god to come. He still hasn't arrived.'

The painter's eyes widened in horror.

'You made fun of my sister. You made her look like a fiend.' Hiranya paused, disgusted. 'She was a beautiful woman and a caring person, but you propagandists only want one thing – to show your black and white. Well, I have news for you: I don't care. Lord Vishnu didn't *get* her. My son did. Somehow, he tricked her and escaped in the nick of time.'

'I remember how our guru, Lord Svarbhanu, would force us to practice every day by putting hot coals in our hands and making us feel the burn. He said it would make us tough, strong enough to fight. We barely had enough ice water to soothe our burns, and she would skip dipping her hand so that I could use all of it.' He came close to the painter, and whispered in a deceptively soft yet menacing tone, 'And you made fun of such a gentle woman.'

Before the painter knew what was happening, Hiranya's hand had torn through his flesh and sinew and shattered bone to pull out his beating heart. His eyes fluttered close and collapsed to the floor of the cell.

He nodded to himself, until his fist clamped inside the painter's chest, feeling the broken bones as he went through, penetrating the flesh to finally pull out the painter's beating heart. Hiranya's hand had turned crimson. The painter's eyes closed and he collapsed.

'Master, there's one more thing I want to tell you,' Kalanemi's spoke up behind him. 'Master Andhaka has arranged a meeting for you with someone. He said the person has information about where the Vishnusena camp might be.'

'Who is it?' Hiranya arched his brows.

Kalanemi smiled.

44

CHENCHEN

Lady Parvati was hurt. Chenchen massaged a mix of ointments over her wounds and then applied some antiseptic cream.

'I don't want him to die,' Parvati said to nobody in particular, watching the ceiling above her.

Chenchen remained quiet.

'I don't know what I want to do with him …' Parvati's voice broke. 'I just know he's my son and I want him to be fine again.'

'I am sure there is Bhringi in him, somewhere,' Chenchen replied, breaking her silence.

'I know.' Parvati smiled as she held Chenchen's hand. 'Thank you for telling me to follow Nara.'

Chenchen stilled. She hadn't wanted to tell Parvati. She had promised Nara that she wouldn't interfere with his actions towards Andhaka, but she couldn't stop. She was a good person. And she saw the good in others.

'I love him,' Chenchen began, 'but he's wrong. And it's not his fault. He can't see the good in people, not the way I do.

I believe everyone should be given a second chance to be a better person. Andhaka hasn't received that opportunity and I really want you to give him that.'

Parvati smiled. 'You are a good friend, Chenchen. Not many would go against the person they love.'

Chenchen nodded. 'Can I ask you something?'

'Yes?'

'What if he doesn't change, my lady?'

The dim light of the candles flickered, illuminating the hollows of Parvati's worried countenance. She blinked slowly, deep in contemplation.

'I don't know. I don't want to think of that possibility,' she saidat last. 'Even if he doesn't, I will not give up on him. I'll make sure I reform him.'

'You really believe he can be a force for good?'

'Yes.' Parvati had tears in her eyes.

Chenchen hugged her, hoping things would go on for the better.

Chenchen entered Nara's tent to find him stitching his wounds himself. With each stitch, he would let out a short yelp of agony before steeling himself for the next jab of the needle. Chenchen came close to help him.

'You were close, I suppose,' she said.

'I was. And he escaped. Just like every time. I won't get another chance with him like this.'

Chenchen could see Nara mourning, so she embraced him tightly. 'I have to tell you something.'

'Yes?'

'I didn't … I didn't lose my husband to the Mlecchas.'

Nara drew back and gazed at her solemnly. 'Then?'

'It was me,' she said, 'I killed him. He was … He hurt me. I allowed him to abuse me for many days until I realized that I couldn't take it any further and I …'

Nara nodded. 'I understand.'

Chenchen was surprised: she was so bitter towards herself, that she had not expected him to be otherwise.

'I wanted to see the good in people and I didn't,' Chenchen said haltingly. 'After … after he was dead, I lived a very morally questionable life until I met you. Everything that has happened since has made me realize people ought to have second chances. I shouldn't have killed my husband. I should have run away. I shouldn't have given in to my anger.'

'Why are you telling me this now?' Nara asked.

She knelt beside him and turned his face towards her own. 'Because I want you to promise me that you will not let anger get the better of you. You are a good man, Nara. But your anger turns you into a violent man and I cannot let that happen. Promise me?'

Nara nodded, struggling to smile as Chenchen kissed him hard. Nara's hands closed around her and he laid her on the carpet, losing within her, their legs tangling, their hands all over each other.

And in that moment of passion, they were one.

45

PRAHLAD

Three days had gone by. He was in the map room, where all the plans were made and strategy decided upon, where Asa liked to spend most of his time. And here he was, stranded with Dhriti by his side, who looking at Asa's personal belongings kept on the table in front of them.

'What should we do about this?' he asked, holding up signet rings and books.

'Keep them.'

Prahlad nodded, for even he didn't feel like disposing them. It was a sad day. Andhaka had escaped, Holika had died. The treaty had turned out to be a trap.

'We can't let this kind of mistake happen again,' Dhriti said. 'Almost fifty of us died that day. Thank Lord Vishnu, we fell back and dispersed.'

'I know. No more treaties. Only plans on how to destroy the empire now.' Prahlad leaned on the chair which used to be Asa's, and before him, Narada's. 'We should relocate.'

'I know. Again. The morale of the entire camp is low, Prahlad. There is no one to lead us. The previous two leaders died horrible deaths. I don't know what to do in this situation. Everyone wants to give up and leave for the outskirts of Illavarti,' she said.

Prahlad nodded. That seemed like an apt solution. 'What would you do?'

'A few years ago, before I joined the Vishnusena, I was a street fighter, an urchin who would fight with anybody. My trainer always told me that if nothing went according to plan, it doesn't nullify the importance of it. If you are felled by a punch, you get back up and you punch back.'

'So, you fall, learn and get up?' Prahlad asked with raised brows. 'A street fighter, eh? You are all-in-one, I assume.'

'I have had a rough time on the streets,' she said. 'I have seen the best of men and the worst of men, and believe me, they have the same smile and they look the same. It's their actionsthat—' She paused abruptly. 'But when I see you, I see a leader. Become the chief. I still have the power to make you that since I was second-in-command to Asa.'

Prahlad clenched his jaw. 'I'm afraid that I'll not be as good as Narada and Asa.'

Dhriti shook her head. 'You'll be better than them.'

Prahlad didn't get the opportunity to think about Dhriti's suggestion, for right then Nara, Chenchen and the Matrikas entered the tent. Nara was the first one to speak.

'Indra wants an alliance with us.'

Nara continued, 'But not to defeat Hiranyakashyap. Rather, to deal with Andhaka. He feels he's a real threat.'

'How did Indra get word to us about the alliance?" Prahlad asked warily.

'Through me,' Brahmani said, raising her hand. 'When I learnt that the Deva camp was close by, I went to meet him. As you know, he created us. Anyway, when he heard how close we had got to Andhaka, he offered to help us.'

'You told him about our location?' Prahlad choked in disbelief. 'You can't just give that away, my lady!'

'Don't worry, it's Lord Indra.'

Prahlad looked over at Dhriti. 'Relocate. Immediately.'

She nodded.

'What is going on?' Brahmani asked, annoyed.

'We can't take any more chances. I'm sure Lord Indra is a good man but—'

Nara grabbed Prahlad's shaking hand and held it firmly. 'Calm down, son. It's fine. I know you are worried. But Indra is on our side. He always has been even though sometimes it may seem otherwise. He's had to be cruel at times, but he's a king.'

Prahlad shakily sighed, closed his eyes and said, 'Has he told you where Andhaka is?'

'Yes,' Brahmani said. 'He's making his way to Yakshlok in a protected carriage. If we go there by sundown when he'll be travelling, we can apprehend him.'

'How did he know?' Prahlad asked.

'What?' Brahmani asked.

'How did he know where Andhaka was?'

'Spies, of course,' Brahmani scoffed.

'And what does he want in return?'

'Our willingness to apprehend him. He doesn't want to waste manpower,' Parvati added.

Prahlad nodded, 'But we should still relocate. You all can go and get Andhaka and do whatever you feel is right with him.'

'I'll go with you too,' Dhriti said.

Prahlad was not comfortable with the idea, but he nodded in agreement for Dhriti knew what she was doing.

'Are you going to be the chief of Vishnusena?' asked Nara.

All the people in the tent looked at him, as if he alone knew the answer to the question, but he didn't.

'I'm too young,' Prahlad replied. 'Is anyone volunteering?'

Brahmani shrugged. 'We are only here for Andhaka.'

Prahlad looked at Nara hopefully. The Simha was lost in thought for a few moments, then he pulled Prahlad outside of the tent, and began to yell for people to gather around him.

'What are you trying to do?' Prahlad asked.

'What I should have done after the entire problem,' Nara replied. 'You deserve to be –'

BOOM!

A huge blast hit the camp out of nowhere. Nara instantly covered Prahlad, holding him down as another blast rent the air, throwing the camp in dSisarray. People began to scatter and scram, while the Matrikas, Chenchen and Dhriti rushed out.

'What is going on?'

Asura soldiers swarmed outside the camp with catapults from which they were throwing balls of fire at the Vishnusena. And leading the charge was Prahlad's father, Hiranyakashyap.

46
NARASIMHA

Another blast. He knew what he had to do. *Protect Prahlad and Chenchen.*

Shielding the boy with his own body, Nara yelled to Chenchen and Dhriti, 'Run!'

The two of them darted towards the woods.

'You need to run too,' Nara said. 'I'll protect you.'

Prahlad nodded and began to sprint forward. Nara turned to see Hiranya slashing through the Vishnusena with his long, sword. With a loud roar, Nara sank his claws into the throats and torsos of the Asura soldiers around him, causing throats and torsos, bringing a bloodbath across the field. He looked back at Prahlad. He had fallen down, with an arrow sticking out of his ankle. Asura soldier closed in on him, heedless of the civilians who were running for their lives.

His heart thudding crazily in his chest, Nara sprinted towards Prahlad and slammed into the soldier closest to the boy and deposited him several yards away. The other soldier brought his blade up to Nara's throat, but he deflected it with his claws. In a lightning quick move, Nara slashed through the Asura's stomach, gutting him mercilessly. The third soldier took one look at his fallen brothers and fled. Nara pounced upon him and brought him down, his claws tearing into skin so that his tendons were visible.

Nara roared again, yelling to Prahlad, 'Stay with me!'

Prahlad went to hold Nara by his trunk as he directed his way towards the woods, where most of the Vishnusena had dispersed. The Matrikas, who had fought valiantly all this while, were also running, for there were too many Asuras.

'I just … I can't …' Prahlad was shivering.

'Hold on tight. Don't worry. We will get out of this safely,' Nara promised.

An Asura soldier came in front of them, Nara slashed his face. Another was relieved of its bones and left on the forest floor.

He had barely take a few steps when an eerily familiar voice stopped him in his tracks. 'You can't run away now, Simha,' it called out hoarsely.

Nara darted at Hiranyakashyap who was walking towards him casually, his army of a hundred Asuras marching behind him.

'It's over. You're done for.' Hiranya laughed, his golden, armour flashing under the bright sunlight. He addressed Prahlad: 'You have done the unforgivable. You have killed your aunt. You are no longer my son.'

'Leave me alone,' Prahlad whispered.

'I can't hear you.'

'Leave me alone!' Prahlad shouted, clutching Nara's torso tightly, as if trying to absorb energy from him.

'Oh boy, I can't do that,' Hiranya scoffed, as he took aim and flung his sword at Nara and Prahlad.

The boy closed his eyes in trepidation, but when he opened them he saw that Nara had stopped the blade in the nick of time. Nara's symbol glowed, shining like a beacon. His hands had turned bloody, but he didn't care. He roared. Setting Prahlad down on the ground, he leapt towards Hiranya, blade poised to attack.

'Oh, you dare to use my weapon against me,' Hiranya mocked as he lunged at the Simha.

As the two combatants crossed paths, Nara stabbed Hiranya with his own sword, taking the Asura king by surprise. The blade pierced through the golden armour and Hiranya groaned. He lashed out at Nara with his foot. Nara grabbed his leg and flipped the Asura king on to his back. He tried to stab Hiranya again, but this time he was the one who landed on his back, slamming against a tree trunk. Despite the pain surging through his body, Nara stood up. The sword was still in his hand. He could see Hiranya walking towards Prahlad, to kill him.

He swung the blade across Hiranya's back, piercing his armour with a definite strike. The Asura king fell. Nara ran to Prahlad and picked him up once more. 'We need to leave now,' he coughed.

But by then, Hiranya was back on his feet. He had pulled out his blade from the armour and was pointing it at Nara.

'Ah, you couldn't have made me angrier. But you just did.'

With a thunderous roar, Hiranya and his army charged at Nara and Prahlad. Suddenly, arrows began to rain down from the sky and on to the Asuras. Hiranya looked up, trying to ascertain where the arrows were coming from. As more and more Asura soldiers succumbed to the assault, only the king stood strong.

'Who is it? Show yourself!' he commanded.

For a moment, Nara thought it was Indra when he noticed the flying machination with two wings, and a dozen similar ones behind it. They looked like bees from the ground up but they were huge vimanas. One of the vimanas flew close to Nara and Prahlad.

'Come on in!' A bright sliver of sunlight obscured Nara's vision as he realized who it was.

Garuda.

47

NARASIMHA

Nara was elated to see his old friend but at the same time he was baffled. While the Asuras were fending off the Suparns, he helped Prahlad into the vimana. With a quick flick, Garuda zoomed above the ground, pulling the vimana upwards when there was a large disturbance. When the vimana didn't climb as high as it ought to, Garuda peered over the side and saw an Asura hanging from the ledge. Nara dug his claws into the soldier's hands. The Asura groaned in pain, released the ledge and fell to his death on the ground below.

'How did you know? Why are you here?' Nara asked his friend, who was busy navigating the woods with unnatural speed.

'You told me we should do the right thing,' Garuda said. 'I couldn't help but feel I should help you after one of my spies at Indra's camp learnt about the Matrikas and how it had all unfolded. This wasn't supposed to happen, the fight and all. I thought you all came in peace, but I didn't know the Asuras would attack today, friend.'

Nara slapped his friend's back. 'Well, I'm glad you are here. We couldn't have survived without you.'

'Ah well, my colleagues were quite grateful for your help in getting the somas to operate our vehicles and cure our health issues. This was the least we could have done in return.' Garuda grinned as he began to drop the vimana down.

'I hope they'll be fine from the Asuras.'

'Oh well, sure. After seeing the situation, we realized this was an evacuation protocol, so we just got you out. By now, they will have dispersed and gone back to their camp. They do all these shenanigans, from time to time.'

'I have been meaning to ask,' Nara said, recalling what Garuda had told him earlier, 'why do you have spies in Indra's camp?'

'Well, I have spies everywhere. It's good to have ears everywhere,' he said with a cheeky smile.

They reached the middle of the forest where Nara helped Prahlad out of the vimana.

'So what now?' asked Garuda.

'We need a way to find our friends,' said Prahlad.

'Friends, eh?' Garuda scoffed. 'Better use your nose now, mate.'

Nara nodded, sniffing; he could clearly smell Chenchen in the woods. 'This way.' He pointed east, and the three of them ventured in deeper.

They had been walking for three hours and the scent was growing stronger. As they walked, Prahlad had told Garuda the entire story and how everyone had come to be at the Vishnusena camp, what they went through and why Hiranyakashyap was hell bent on killing them.

They finally reached a clearing, where Nara saw two Asura soldiers with their swords, scanning the vicinity.

'Shhh, they must be the scouts sent out,' whispered Nara. 'Let me handle them.'

He went forward, claws ready to attack them, when the soldiers turned, bringing their blades towards Nara. More soldiers came out of nowhere, as if they were waiting to ambush them. Prahlad and Garuda were pushed out of the bushes and into the clearing, to join Nara. Even as the Asuras debated what to do with them, a flurry of arrows came to their rescue. Someone threw a noose around an Asura's neck and made quick work of him. Before long, the Asuras that had ambushed them were dead.

'Missed us?'

Nara turned to see Brahmani, Parvati, Chamunda and the other Matrikas along with Dhriti and Chenchen. They all greeted each other, while Garuda stood by himself a short distance away.

'Yep, no need to greet and meet the person who saved your ungrateful asses,' he muttered.

Nara laughed and turned away from his friends, introducing Garuda to everyone.

'It's nice to meet you,' Chenchen said as Garuda bowed dramatically. 'We are all hiding in a nearby cave. We should go and plan our next move.'

Nara hoped whatever plan they came up with now would be the last one to end this once and for all.

48

PRAHLAD

Nara, Chenchen, the Matrikas, Dhriti and Garuda stood in a circle under the high ceiling of the dripping cave, waiting for Prahlad to begin. Time was of essence – the Asura soldiers would be searching for them in these corners of the woods. Prahlad knew he had to act quickly.

For a boy who was about to turn fifteen, Prahlad had faced a lot of pressure in the past year. There were Vishnusena survivors outside, trying to form a camp out of the necessities that they had brought from their previous camp. Not many had survived. One more attack and they would probably perish.

'We need to make it clear. From here on, whatever we do, we have to succeed,' Prahlad said sternly and everyone nodded.

'Lady Brahmani,' he continued, 'You must carry on with your plan as decided. Track down Andhaka. You might have a few hours more to actually act on it. The sun is about to go down and it'll be twilight for the next few hours.'

She nodded.

'Dhriti, are you still going?' Prahlad asked the redhead.

'Yes.'

'Me too,' Chenchen volunteered. 'I came here for my friend, Parvati,' she said, patting the queen's back, 'I will make sure she finds Andhaka.'

Nara smiled and so did Prahlad. All this war and bloodshed had brought people closer.

'Lord Garuda,' Prahlad said, with a heavy heart, 'I would request you to take the survivors outside, to your camp.'

Garuda was surprised but he crossed his arms over his chest and nodded. 'Sure, I would love to have some company other than my men, kid. I hope they don't mind the bunch of squawking fiends that my people are.'

Prahlad chuckled. 'I'm sure they won't. If I succeed in doing what I plan to do, I will be able to round up everyone in the kingdom.'

'And what do you plan to do?' Dhriti asked.

Prahlad clenched his jaw, recalling what Holika had told him, moments before her death. 'For that, I need to speak to Nara alone.'

Brahmani nodded. 'Best of luck, kid.'

One after another, they patted his shoulder encouragingly and left the cave. Garuda began to make arrangements for people to leave while Brahmani called for Chenchen and the Matrikas to leave.

Dhriti remained frozen. 'What do you intend to do?'

'That is something between me and Nara,' Prahlad said, squeezing her shoulders gently. 'Don't worry. It'll work. I'm sure it will.'

'You're scaring me.'

He smiled. 'It was a privilege being with you.' I don't know if I told you but turning to the Vishnusena, it happened partially because of you. You gave me the strength to believe in something greater than this universe. Thank you.'

Dhriti didn't smile or embrace him. She just broke his gaze and ran from the cave. Prahlad felt Nara's strong palm over his shoulder.

'Are you okay, boy?'

'How can *you* be fine in this dire situation?' he turned to the Simha, who was beaten up just as badly, but still had the energy to fight on.

'So, what is the plan?'

Prahlad sighed, not knowing if he ought to believe Holika. *Could she be telling the truth?*

'You must have noticed the armour and the weapon my father is using,' he said.

Nara nodded. 'What is that thing?' He looked at his hands, which were bandaged up, crimson seeping through the white layers.

'It's not of this world. And while he's wearing it, he is invincible. But there's a way to defeat him,' Prahlad said, hesitant to smile.

'A way?'

'Yes, but for that to work, you need to navigate through the sewers.'

'And go where?'

Prahlad looked outside the cave. *Only a few hours left.*

'If my calculations are right, you need to be in the palace. Find a hiding spot.' Prahlad said grimly. 'I'm done running from him. It's time to be smart and believe that Lord Vishnu will help us succed.' He looked at the symbol that Nara carried on his chest.

'Me too. I believe he will help us this time,' said Nara.'

An hour later, Nara found himself outside the city gates. Without protection, men or weapons. He was not afraid any more. *It is now or never. It will be over soon. It has to be*, he repeated to himself. Chanting Lord Vishnu's name, he walked on the drawbridge that was opened up and the guards on the gates noticed a figure moving towards them casually.

Prahlad was in a loose tunic and a dirty dhoti. He was barefoot. Judging by his appearance, no one could even say that he was ever a prince. Alarmed, the guards pointed their weapons at Prahlad but he continued walking.

'Stand back! Who are you?' Suddenly the guard's face contorted into shock. 'Why, if it isn't the bloody traitor!'

Prahlad raised his arms in surrender. He looked up at the windows in the gate where the large crossbows were aimed at him.

'I don't want any trouble,' Prahlad said. 'I just want to go and meet my father.'

'What are you saying?' asked the Asura.

Prahlad, with a grudge in his heart, replied, 'I have come to give myself up.'

49
NARASIMHA

There were three Asuras guarding the sewer. Nara cursed under his breath, and sprinted towards the guards, surprising them with raw tenacity as he quickly swiped his claws on one guard's chest and broke the second's jaw. The third used his shield to ward off the Simha's punishing blows. But Nara somersaulted over him, toppling him into the dark, dirty water and then proceeded to suffocate him until he gave up on his life.

And then he felt a force from the back.

He fell over the water, the black water splashing over his face and dirtying his body. He tried to loosen the grasp that. Had grabbed him from behind and he was pushed down on the ground, with the lock as firm and tight as possible.

He instantly pushed himself back, his feet springing in action while his arms tousling with pain. He was on his feet, while the grasp of the man was still on him.

Nara was pushed himself in the back and shoved the guard who held him against the wall.

There was a loud cry and wail as the grasp was loosened. Nara got free and with a sigh of relief and a stab of tension, he turned to see the third guard who had sprung up on him while he was killing the other guards.

This one was larger in size and he had two big burly arms from which he came forward. He didn't want to use the blade he carried, probably because he wanted to hurt Nara with his palms to showoff his skills.

But Nara was quick, as he turned around with a swift motion when the guard came and he rounded himself in the back of the guard.

Being a physician, he knew the positioning of the cervical spine of the soldier and thus he punched where it was needed.

At that moment, the guard screamed in agony and fell on the gutter water himself. He tried to struggle, but Nara kicked him with his feet and twisted his neck so he remained where he was for an indefinite time.

Nara walked into the sewer pipe which was twice his size but quite narrow, noticing a stream of dirty, dark water flowing under his feet. He didn't have much time. Probably fifteen minutes to reach the palace halls. He consulted the paper he had in his hand to see the directions that Dhriti had mapped for him.

He began walking through the pipes, his eyes moving rapidly up and down from the paper to the front, where the darkness lay. His steps were accompanied by the sound of the gushing water and the nauseating smell of rats and shit. Nara quickly turned the last right and dashed forward until he reached a shattered gate which he crouched and went under. He crossed two sewer gates that would open to the city, but he wanted to reach the one that led to the palace.

He remembered what Prahlad had told him: 'When you reach the sewers, make sure you don't get distracted. And you have to reach the palace before me. We don't have time. So, hurry.'

And he did, finally reaching the last gate marked on his map. He climbed the gate and broke through the circular drain. Dirty and stinking, he staggered out of the drain and into the sweet-smelling wine cellar, he went to the exit, where he saw a guard on duty.

I'm in the palace. Thank the gods!

He noticed the guard was on the other side of the corridor, so he slipped out and tiptoed towards the throne hall where Prahlad had told him to go.

I'm close. I hope he is as well.

50

CHENCHEN

As the horse whinnied, she held on to her stomach.

I didn't tell him.

She wished she had but she knew tat she could tell him when all this was over. That would be the best time. She glanced at the mare next to her, which Dhriti rode. Dhriti noticed Chenchen's worried face, but chose to ignore it, looking ahead instead. They were approaching their destination – all on their horses, riding against the desert wind. It was in the outskirts of the southern plains and was moving towards the more deserted plain of Illavarti.

Chenchen couldn't believe that she had started out as a doctor who had never risked her life, yet here she was, in every mission, facing risks and helping her friends. She had changed a lot and she was glad.

As they reached a dune-like structure, Brahmani, who was in front, stopped everyone. She pulled out a spyglass and looked through it. Even Chenchen brought out her spyglass and observed the goings-on in the distance. There were two carriages, but stationary. Two men were standing, checking the wheels.

'Indra said that they would be here,' Brahmani said. 'Their carriage must have stopped because of the plains. Often, the wheels get ruddy on these bloody roads.' She looked back at her companions. 'Everyone! Let's make this our final fight.'

And she rode on, with her noose slapping against her thigh, with Chamunda and the other Matrikas following right behind her.

Dhriti and Chenchen were riding in the back. 'When do you plan to tell him?' she asked.

Chenchen clenched her jaw, 'Soon. I'm just ... I don't know how he will take it.'

'I'm sure he will be happy.' Dhriti smiled.

'We aren't even officially married and I'm already pregnant,' Chenchen cursed under her breath. 'But then, we didn't have time time either.'

'I'm sure, everything will fall in place,' Dhriti said calmly.

Chenchen hoped so. She really did. She rode further, through the heavy blizzard of the desert to reach the chariots where the men continued to work, seemingly oblivious to their arrival. All of them dismounted, their feet sinking in the sand. Chenchen and Brahmani walked towards the chariot. The men still didn't move.

Curious, Chenchen grabbed the Asura guard by the shoulder and turned him around. To her shock, it was a puppet made of bamboo and straw,.

'What the ...'

Chenchen glanced at the astonished Dhriti, and then at Brahmani, who had made the same discovery.

She walked around to the door of the chariot, Parvati on her heels, and pulled it open. There was no one inside.

'This is not good,' Chenchen said, turning to Parvati. 'We have been fooled.'

All of a sudden, people began to surround them. Parvati and Chenchen stared at the men. They weren't Asuras, but Manavs with skin like Chenchen's and Parvati's. They were armed with crossbows and they bore the symbol of a rising elephant in the middle of their armour.

And through the dust storm, in clear view, the women saw the man responsible – Indra.

51

PRAHLAD

He was bound and gagged as he was taken through the streets of Kashyapuri, pushed and shoved around like he had been before. But this time, the people were not against him. They were hollering for him. He could hear men and women shouting that after the Holika incident, they believed in Lord Vishnu and wanted to follow Prahlad's path.

Prahlad's chest was bursting with elation.

He had dozens of soldiers around him while the other soldiers were trying to control the riotous public who had frying pans and wooden clubs. They wanted to fight the soldiers who were holding them back.

'It's been a while,' said a guard next to Prahlad. 'They are not satisfied with the ruling government.'

Prahlad nodded. He had never expected his administrative failures to result in an incitement of the public. He walked towards the long, white marble staircase that led to the golden palace of the Asura king, where his seat as a prince of Kashyapuri used to be. As he climbed the last step, he looked back to see thousands of people being jostled back by the soldiers, who were waiting for them to do something.

Prahlad raised his arms. In response, the people rejoiced and jumped, clamouring loudly. He smiled until he was pushed around by the guard and thrown inside the palace. Behind him, the gates closed on the people's cries. He looked up and the first thing he saw was a long carpet laid with a thick red carpet and flanked by massive columns on either side.

At the other end of the carpet, his father sat on the throne. Since it was twilight, he wasn't wearing his armour. He was vulnerable, just like Prahlad had expected him to be.

'One can only wonder why the traitor has returned,' Hiranya said, his voice booming in the hall. He stepped down from the throne and walked towards Prahlad with a mace in his hand. He didn't have his weapon either. 'What made you change your mind? Why have you come back? Do you want to be my son again?'

Prahlad said nothing. His heart was racing. 'I never planned to disobey you, father. But you forced my hand. You have ruled this kingdom in a corrupt manner.'

'And what way is the right way?'

'The way towards peace.'

'Peace is non-existent in this current society. We have no use for it.'

Prahlad shook his head, his eyes locked on Hiranya, who was still yards away from him. He feared that if his father came any closer, he would be hit by the mace, but suddenly he felt the fear leave his mind, for he knew in his heart that Lord Vishnu would save him.

'I never wanted to kill you,' Prahlad said. 'But you had left me no choice.'

'What do you mean?'

'I saw what you did to the people, my people. You wanted to kill me with such blood-thirst. It was madness, father. You cannot be allowed to live,' Prahlad said. 'Even if you are imprisoned, you are bound to escape with that armour and weapon.'

Hirany a scoffed, 'Wait, hold on. You stand before me, bound, in *my* palace, *my* kingdom, yet you claim that *you* have the power to let me live? It is I who am allowing you to live! Not you, boy.'

'It is Lord Vishnu who is allowing us to live. And Lord Vishnu will protect me.'

'Lord Vishnu?' Hiranya laughed derisively. 'Where is he? Might I know, is he here?' he asked, pointing at a pillar. He hefted the mace and hit the column with it, shattering it. 'I don't think he's here. This is just rubble.'

I hope he comes soon. Nara – where are you?

'Lord Vishnu is *everywhere*,' Prahlad said with a brave, stern face. 'He's in everything, even the pillars.'

'So you are saying he's here?' Hiranya pointed at another column. 'I'm sure he is here. Where else would he be, right?'

Once more, he smashed the mace into another pillar, decimating it. The ceiling began to crack in places.

Hiranya came closer to Prahlad, and then walked to the pillar next to him. 'If he's not here, then he's not anywhere. Your Lord Vishnu doesn't exist,' the Asura king thundered.

'He never did and he never will. Stop believing in these fantasies, boy!'

Nara ...where are you? Oh by Lord Vishnu, protect me!

Prahlad closed his eyes in fear as Hiranya raised the mace once more. Seconds passed. When he opened his eyes, he saw Hiranya wrestling with a shadowy figure.

Prahald stepped back, realizing it was Narasimha who had taken the Asura king by surprise and wrested his mace away.

Hiranya scowled and began to chant something.

'You can't summon it.' Prahlad laughed. 'Look outside.'

'But you can't kill me either!'

'Not by a man or beast, or outside or inside, or heaven or earth,' Prahlad recited.

Hiranya gasped. 'How did you—'

Before he could voice his shock, Nara grabbed him by the throat. The Asura fought back but in vain.

Nara was too strong. The Shrivatsa glowed on his chest as he dragged Hiranya to the door and kicked it open. The guards scattered, fearing for their lives; none dared intervene to save their king. Nara bent Hiranya over his folded knees and snapped his spine in two. The Asura king let out a piercing cry of agony.

As he flailed about for purchase, he managed to scratch the Simha's face, but Nara barely felt it. Putting his razor-sharp claws together, he ripped open Hiranya's torso, an pulled out his innards.

Thus did Hiranyakashyap meet his end: neither inside, nor outside; neither on the ground, nor in the sky; neither in the morning, nor at night. He died across a threshold, in Narasimha's lap, at twilight. Right then, with the grieving boy as its only witness, the reign of the tyrannical Asura bloodline came to an end.

Prhlad couldn't believe it was over. Even after seeing his father's mangled, lifeless body, he remained disbelieving.

It was actually done. A tremor went through his body, ending in a tearful jerk of sorrow. He felt compelled to shed copious tears and howl loud enough for the world to hear. He hadn't expected to feel such overwhelming sadness.

But he did.

After all, he had killed his father. It had been the stuff of dreams all this while, but now that the deed had been done, it took on a nightmarish quality. As he hugged himself to hold his emotions in check, he felt Nara's thick, burly arms wrap around him like a father's – a father that he had always wanted.

And as he held on to himself hugging himself, Nara's thick arms wrapped around him like a father. A father that Prahlad always strove to have.

'I am sorry,' Nara said.

'It had to be done.' He hugged him tightly. 'It had to be done.'

52

PARVATI

She knew there was trouble looming when they found the puppets. And it became worse when they realized it was an ambush.

Brahmani was the only one who wasn't frightened; she managed to assess their situation dispassionately. at the entire situation. 'What is the meaning of this, Indra?'

The caped man in the silver armour towered over them. His moustache and hair were trimmed short and he looked different. This was the first time Parvati was seeing Indra in this avatar.

'Oh, girls, don't take it personally.' Indra shrugged. 'Nothing to do with all of you. The only reason you lot are here is because of her.'

Parvati was shocked to see he was pointing at Chenchen. 'What did she do?' Parvati demanded.

'She is the lover of a doomed man.' Indra sighed. 'I should have killed her when I first saw her, but I didn't because I liked Nara. Until he did the unforgivable.'

'And what did he do?' Parvati asked.

Cold, calm eyes met Parvati's terrified ones. 'He killed my son.'

A tremor went through Parvati's body, to the point that she glanced at Chenchen who didn't know herself.

'He can't ...' Chenchen choked.

'Well, unfortunately, he did.' Indra shook his head mournfully. 'I know. I wanted to take away what he loves most.' His urge to take what he loves the most,' his icy glare continued to torment Chenchen. He didn't look calm any more. 'In fact, my son's death was the only reason I formed a treaty with Andhaka and Hiranyakashyap. It was all because of Andhaka. He wanted to do one last deed, before leaving for his ancestral home.'

'When did he go?' Parvati asked, flaring her nostrils.

'Oh, last night. When I learnt you were planning on inducting her into the ranks of the Matrikas, I lied to Brahmani so she could bring Chenchen with her. Sadly, she won't be leaving with you.

'And since you all are here, I can't let any one of you, leave, right? Because I don't want you to come and seek revenge after I let you go. So off you all go to die!'

And with that, he walked back into the dust storm. Parvati didn't wait. With a quick flick, she readied her bow and arrow and began shooting at the Manav soldiers. Within moments the other Matrikas joined in. But the Manavs released a barrage of arrows. Parvati was hit twice – once in the chest and then in the shoulder, and she fell back. Everything was a blur for a while but she didn't stay down. She got to her feet and shot as many arrows as possible, until her quiver was empty.

With a heavy breath, she fell on the ground. She looked at the Matrikas – they all had arrows lodged in their bodies except for Chamunda who had deflected the attacks with the trident. They all were struggling to survive the ambush. She looked at Dhriti, who was slumped against the carriage, next to the puppet, with an arrow in her knee.

Chamunda went into the desert, to search for Indra and returned to say. 'He's gone. The bastard has gone.'

Parvati sighed, 'We survived it, eh?' she said to Chenchen, who was in her peripheral vision. There was no response. 'Chenchen?'

She turned to see her friend and found her lying next to the chariot with an arrow right through her skull, her eyes dull and lifeless. Parvati took n Chenchen in her arms. 'No, no you can't … no!'

The Matrikas came forward, and gasped in horror, 'She can't … die … she can't …'

Tears began to trickle down Parvati's cheeks and fall on the lifeless body of her friend. This was all because of Indra and his scheming ways. She knew whose fault it was. She had always known but was too blind to see it.

She looked up at the Matrikas. 'I was wrong. Andhaka,' she said, nodding to herself, as if acknowledging it would make it real. 'Andhaka is not Skanda.'

The Matrikas remained silent.

'No,' Parvati added with finality, 'he is no son of mine. He is evil. And what do we do with evil? We slaughter it.'

53

NARASIMHA

He looked at the burning pyre where Chenchen's body lay. His arms were crossed tightly and he felt nothing. There was neither anger nor frustration. He was just numb.

He had never felt like this in his life. He had cried his heart out when he first saw her, after returning from the triumphant win over Hiranyakashyap. When one evil ended, a new tragedy struck, as if someone didn't want his happiness to last.

He knew her death was because of his karma. He had done so many horrible acts that they had caused this. His past wouldn't let him redeem himself. He would be always a killer.

Might as well continue to be that than be a good person.

'She was carrying your child,' Dhriti confided in him when he sat down, shell-shocked.

His child. He wanted to cry longer, louder, but he glanced at Garuda and the Suparn army behind him, the Matrikas, Dhriti and finally at Prahlad beside him.

'She was a great woman,' he said. 'A great person, in fact.'

Nara tightened his jaw, 'What is the status of the city?'

'We can talk about it later. It's been only three days. You can take time to mourn.'

'I don't want to,' Nara rasped. 'Answer me. What is the status of the city?'

'The people are rioting. There is a power vacuum. The remaining Asura soldiers are being rounded up as we speak,' replied Prahlad.

'And what do you plan to do?'

'Go back. Bring peace. I think they all look up to me now,' said Prahlad.

'And where is Andhaka?'

'No one knows. Just like the last time, he has escaped,' Prahlad said. 'He's up to something, though.'

Nara nodded. 'And I am assuming we don't know where Indra is?'

'He has left his last encampment. He has probably gone back to Devlok since he's the only ruler of Illavarti now. He will be sending his army soon to bring Kashyapuri down. But we can't let that happen,' Prahlad said firmly. 'It's still our city and we shall fight back.'

Nara nodded. 'We shall. So, who is going to command this army, this kingdom?'

Prahlad said, 'I was thinking I would take charge.'

Nara shook his head. 'It can't be you.'

He looked at Prahlad with bitterness in his eyes. He was done entrusting his duty to others.

'Then?'

Nara looked at the funeral pyre, his thoughts on the antyeshti that had been done for Chenchen, and a host of emotions swam through him. His anger and frustration overflowed. He no longer wanted to serve. He knew he wouldn't be able to cut off Indra's head and gouge his lifeless eyes out while being just a soldier in another empire. In order to defeat them, he had to become like them – like Andhaka and Indra.

'No,' said Nara, looking at the timid boy. 'It will be me. I will be the king of Kashyapuri.'

TO BE CONTINUED ...
IN
THE NARASIMHA TRILOGY BOOK 3
PRAHLAD

ABOUT THE AUTHOR

Kevin Missal is a twenty-two year old graduate of St. Stephen's College. His first book, book one in the Kalki Trilogy, *Dharmayoddha Kalki: Avatar of Vishnu* was released in 2017, and garnered critical praise. It was termed '2017's mythological phenomenon' and was a national bestseller.

Kevin loves reading, watching films and building stories in his mind. He lives in New Delhi and you can contact him at: kevin.s.missal@gmail.com

ALSO BY
KEVIN MISSAL

Narasimha, once a brave soldier, has left the war and lies
low as a physician in a village. But a familiar face from his
past seeks his help to stop the tyranny of the blind usurper
Andhaka. If Narasimha refuses, the world might just end. What
will he do? And why did he leave the war in the first place?
Prahlad, the interim king of Kashyapuri, is torn between the
ideals of his unrighteous father and his love for Lord Vishnu.
Whom will he choose?
Hiranyakashyap, the ruler of the Asura Empire, wants to
avenge the death of his wife. To do that, he must go through
the Trials and get the ultimate weapon - the Brahmastra.
But the Trials have sent so many others to their death. Can
Hiranyakashyap survive?
Welcome to the reimagining of the fourth Avatar of Lord
Vishnu by bestselling author Kevin Missal.